BEBES PRECIOSOS

5001 HISPANIC BABY NAMES

ROSE MARIE ARCE
and **MAITÉ JUNCO**

If you purchased this book without a cover, you should be aware that this book is stolen property. It was reported as "unsold and destroyed" to the publisher, and neither the author nor the publisher has received any payment for this "stripped book."

BEBES PRECIOSOS: 5,001 HISPANIC BABY NAMES is an original publication of Avon Books. This work has never before appeared in book form.

AVON BOOKS
A division of
The Hearst Corporation
1350 Avenue of the Americas
New York, New York 10019

Copyright © 1995 by Rose Marie Arce and Maité Junco
Published by arrangement with the authors
Library of Congress Catalog Card Number: 94-96860
ISBN: 0-380-77843-2

All rights reserved, which includes the right to reproduce this book or portions thereof in any form whatsoever except as provided by the U.S. Copyright Law. For information address Acton, Dystel, Leone & Jaffe, 79 Fifth Avenue, New York, New York 10003.

First Avon Books Printing: August 1995

AVON TRADEMARK REG. U.S. PAT. OFF. AND IN OTHER COUNTRIES, MARCA REGISTRADA, HECHO EN U.S.A.

Printed in the U.S.A.

RA 10 9 8 7 6 5 4 3 2 1

WHAT'S IN A NAME?

A boy called *Agni* is named for the *God of Fire* and *Abigail* is *Her father's joy*.

A baby girl born in January might be named *Bertilia* or *Marcela* and a boy born in December may be called *Amado* or *Anastasio*.

What ever meaning you wish to attach to your child's name, **BEBES PRECIOSOS** will give you a wide selection for both boys and girls.

ABOUT THE AUTHORS OF *BEBES PRECIOSOS*

MAITÉ JUNCO was named after two of the Catholic Church's most important saints, *Maria* and *Teresa*, but, to make her name something special, her mother insisted on the nickname *Maité*, the Basque word for *I love you*.

ROSE MARIE ARCE was named for her country's patron saint, *Rosa of Lima, Peru*. Because her family had an affinity for French names she converted her name to *Rose Marie*.

Avon Books are available at special quantity discounts for bulk purchases for sales promotions, premiums, fund raising or educational use. Special books, or book excerpts, can also be created to fit specific needs.

For details write or telephone the office of the Director of Special Markets, Avon Books, Dept. FP, 1350 Avenue of the Americas, New York, New York 10019, 1-800-238-0658.

Our thanks to the Latina mothers who named us, Miny and Haydeé, and to the friends who helped us compile these names, particularly Michael Rohrer and Marta Jalil. We are also grateful to our agent, Jane Dystel; our editor, Gwen Montgomery; and our friend Lisa Wager.

Contents

Abbreviations
ix
Introduction
xi

PART I:
Names for Girls /
Nombres de Niñas
1

Part II:
Names for Boys /
Nombres de Niños
99

PART III
Saints' Names by Day /
Nombres de Santos por Día
211

Bibliography
237

Abbreviations

Af	African	*masc*	masculine
Arab	Arabian	*Myth*	Mythology
Celt	Celtic	*Nig*	Nigerian
Comb	Combination	*Nor*	Norwegian
dim	diminutive	*OE*	Old English
Egypt	Egyptian	*OF*	Old French
Eng	English	*OG*	Old German
fem	feminine	*Per*	Persian
Fr	French	*Pol*	Polish
Gael	Gaelic	*Port*	Portuguese
Ger	German	*Rus*	Russian
Gr	Greek	*Scan*	Scandinavian
Heb	Hebrew	*Scot*	Scottish
It	Italian	*Sp*	Spanish
Jap	Japanese	*Var*	variant
Lat	Latin	*Tib*	Tibetan

Introduction

Guillermina Sara Rogelia Galletti de Junco named her daughter, the author, after two of the Catholic Church's most important saints, María (the mother of God) and Teresa (St. Teresa of Avila), but because she wanted her only daughter to be called something special, she also insisted on the nickname Maité, the Basque word for "I love you." Haydeé Cecilia Boero de Weiler wanted her daughter to bear the name of her country's patron saint, Rosa of Lima, Peru. But because her family had an affinity for French names, she converted it to Rose Marie. One woman was from Cuba; the other was born in Peru. Yet both our mothers, like many Latina mothers, looked to their people's dominant religion, Catholicism, to name their children, and combined it with a Latino flair for the exotic or different.

Other mothers choose the names of the saints or biblical figures who share their child's birth date. They look for significant religious events or to religious figures important to their home country, like Guadalupe of Mexico. Some saints' names are chosen because the saint committed an act of kindness or had a penchant for something the parents liked, such as Saint Martin's affection for animals.

There are saints chosen because they were first or last born, as was the new baby, or because of their special relationship with their biblical parents.

As a way of making these religious names more interesting, many Latinos look to alter the spelling or combine them with more modern names. Parents flip through gossip magazines in search of movie and soap opera stars, such as Mexican actress María Félix and TV talk show host Cristina. Fathers seem particularly partial to sports figures, such as Roberto Clemente, the baseball giant, or boxer Julio César Chávez. They can also honor celebrities such as Raúl Julia or Antonio Banderas of the movies or Federico Peña, the Secretary of Transportation. There are always a great number of singers to choose from, such as Celia Cruz, Gloria Estefan, or Plácido Domingo. And historical figures abound, such as Simón Bolívar, the liberator of much of Latin America, or more recently Augusto Sandino, the Nicaraguan rebel.

When those options don't work, there are always more simple, descriptive names available. A child with strong physical characteristics, such as being very blond, can be named for the trait, as in Blanca or Rubio. Moral qualities the child could aspire to, such as Pura or Justo (Pure and Just), are possibilities. Since many Latinos are still fresh from the experience of immigration, they can always recall their homeland or hometown by choosing a name such as Salvador, for El Salvador. If their dream is to see their child aspire to a particular profession, they may prod the baby by choosing a name like Pastor (clergyman).

Latinos living in the United States have a particularly difficult time because a child raised here will in all likelihood use his or her name socially and professionally in an American environment. Parents therefore have to consider whether the name they choose will be properly pronounced and understood or whether its meaning will be lost and its sound mangled. Parents should decide whether they mind that many of their child's friends may have trouble pronouncing Guillermina or Heriberto.

They also have to consider whether the name is likely to be translated by well-meaning schoolmates and whether that translation results in a reasonable name. If a child is named Ernesto, there is a good chance some people will insist on calling him Ernie or Ernest, and Rafael can easily become Ralph. In many entries in this book, a possible English translation has been given in parentheses at the end of the description to help you consider the implications. Parents should also watch out for names with double meanings such as Fátima, which sounds like fat.

Even with all these precautions, there are certainly families that would choose a name for its personal significance, for example, paying regard to a deceased relative or close friend. Some families insist on giving all their first-born sons and daughters the same name or honoring an important relative, such as a grandfather. In those cases the child may someday want to know the various interpretations of his or her name or may look to alter it by using a nickname.

This book provides many options in all these categories, from significant saints (including their birth dates or days on which they are remembered) to Hispanic luminaries. There are also diminutives and nicknames for each and new names formed by the combination of older ones, such as Adaluz. If a name is truly out of use, it has been omitted, but names with somewhat negative connotations have been kept so you can consider the implication of naming a child after a patricidal mythological character or a crazy person. There are a good number of very American names, too, in case you want to opt for something that just sounds okay with a Hispanic surname.

There are projections that by the next century a good fifth to a quarter of America's residents will have some Latino roots. The more of us there are, the more our names will resonate in this country. Our names are already in newspapers and history books, on television and in movies, in state capitals and in Washington. As time passes more Americans will also take our names as we have taken theirs. All this makes it easier for mothers and fathers to do what ours once did: to comfortably name their children something rich that has special meaning to them.

BEBES PRECIOSOS

5001
HISPANIC BABY NAMES

I

Names for Girls

Nombres de Niñas

A

Abigail Heb. "Her father's joy." From "ab" for father and "guilah" for joy, this is the name of a biblical figure who was Nabal's widow, then David's new wife.
Abi, Abil, Gaila

Abril Lat. Second month of the ancient Roman Calendar (the year began with March). Spanish actress Victoria Abril.
Abrila, Avril, Avrila

Acacia Gr. Name of a blossoming tree that symbolized resurrection.
Cacia

Ada Heb. "Happy." Biblical figure, wife of Lamec and mother of Jabel and Jubal.
Adi, Adia, Adina, Adita, Aditi, Aida, Aidita

Adabela Combination of **Ada** and **Bella**, happiness and beauty.
Adabelle, Adabelita, Bela

Adalgisa Ger. "Noble hostage." Italian saint remembered April 20. The lance of the nobility.

Adalia Per. "Divinity of Fire." Biblical figure, daughter of Aman, who died on the gallows with her mother. "The daughter of fire." Derived from Ada and Lia.

3

Adaluz Combination of **Ada,** "happy," and luz, "light."
Adalucy, Lucita, Lucy, Luz

Adamantina Var. of **Diamantina,** the dim. of diamond.
Ada, Tina, Tini

Adela Ger. "Of noble lineage." Saint, abbess, daughter of the king of Australia, Dagoberto II, who the Catholic church remembers on September 8 and December 24. She is brave and takes risks, but stands by her principles.
Adelina, Adelinda, Adilia, Adelis, Adelita (Adelle)

Adelaida Ger. "Noble princess." Made for sainthood, wife of Lotario II of Lombard. While princess she contributed to the conversion of the slaves and while she was never formally canonized, her feast is celebrated in the German diocese on December 16.
Adela, Adelia, Adelina

Adelfa Gr. "Beloved sister."
(Adelpha)

Adelina Ger. "Noble, nobility."
Adalina, Alina, Dalina, Deli, Delina, Lina

Adelinda Teut. "Noble, sweet." Comb. form **Adela** and **Linda.**
Adelicia, Edelina

Adeltrudis Ger. From **Ada,** "noble lineage," "beloved," and true, so loved for her nobility.

Adelma Ger. (fem. **Adelmo**) "Old." The bishop of Sherborne in England and the first Englishman to write Latin verse.

Adelrisa Ger. From **Adal,** "of noble lineage," and *wis,* "sage or expert," meaning "sage for the nobility."
Adela, Risa

Adena Heb. "The delicate, small."
Adina —It.-Heb. Dim. **Ada** or a Hebrew name for Gentile.
Adi, Aida, Dina, Dinna, Dinorah
Adolfina (fem. **Adolfo**) "Noble Wolf." Chinese martyr remembered in China on July 9.
Adoración Lat. "Reveres and honors God." Recalls the wise men's trip to see the baby Jesus in Bethlehem, Epiphany celebration January 6.
Adriana Lat. (fem. **Adrian**) Born in Adria, the city of the sea, the woman of the Adriatic Sea, the city of Italy that gave its name to the Adriatic Sea. Crazy and extravagant, remembered on September 8.
Adri, Adria, Adrianna, Adrienne, Ana (Adrien)
Afra Lat. Old form of Africana. Saint and martyr of ancient cultures. One touched by the sun.
Afri, Afrita, Aphra
Afrodita Gr. "Born from the foam of the sea." Aphrodite, goddess of love and beauty.
(Aphrodite)
Agapita Gr. (fem. **Agapito**)
Agape
Agar Heb. "The one who ran away." Egyptian servant of Abraham, who was offered to him by his wife Sarah, who was sterile, so she could bear his successor.
Ágata Gr. (fem. **Agatón**) Two martyrs of the Catholic church, Agata Kim and Agata Lin, remembered September 21 and February 17. She is sublime.
(Agatha)
Aglaé Gr. "The splendid, the radiant, the beauty." Aglaia, one of the three graces in Greek mythology.
Agni Hindi. In Hindu mythology, she was the god of fire.
Agripina Lat. (fem. **Agripino**) Agrippina, daughter of Agrippa, wife of Germanicus Caesar, and

mother of Caligula, saint, virgin and martyr. Very revered in Sicily, her feast is celebrated on June 23.

Agostina Lat. Var. **Augustina** or **Agusta**.
(Augustine)

Agueda Gr. "She is sublime and virtuous." Var. **Ágata**. Saint, virgin, and martyr of Sicilian origin, remembered February 5.

Agustina Lat. (fem. **Agustín**) "The venerated one."
Agi, Agostina, Agusta

Aída Lat. "The distinguished one." The female lead in the opera of the same name by Giuseppe Verdi (1871).
(Ida)

Aideé Var. **Haydeé**. (Heidi)

Ailen Chile. "The live coal." From the Mapuche Indians.
Ailee, Ailene, Aleen, Alene, Aline, Allie, Auleen, Eileen, Ileana, Ileanna, Ilene, Iliana, Ilane, Illena, Leana, Leanalu, Leanna, Lena, Liana, Lianna, Lina
(Eileen)

Ailín Chile. "She is fair and transparent." From the Mapuche Indians.

Aimé Chile. "A bit of something." From the Mapuche Indians.

Aire Gr. *Myth.* Wife of the Moon and father of the Mist. Personified in Ether, means "the purest air."

Aixa Arab. Aishah, the third wife of Muhammad. Name introduced in Spain during Arab occupation and appears in Spanish literature of Pedro de Alarcón, Francisco Villaespesa and Enrique Larreta.

Alaide A contraction of **Adelaida,** a noble princess.

Alana Celt. (fem. **Alan** or **Alano**) "Harmony."

Alba Lat. "Aurora." Name given as a title to a family of Spain's nobility. White and radiant like the dawn, fair-skinned.

Albana Lat. (fem. **Albano**) "From the house of Alba, from the light."
Alba, Albanita

Albertina Ger. (fem. **Albert**) "Eternally brilliant." More common than **Alberta**. She is so noble she glitters.

Albina Lat. (fem. **Albino**) "Of clear complexion."
Albi

Alcestes Gr. Alcestis, heroic wife of Admetus, who offered to die instead of him. She went to Hades and Hercules got her out.

Alcina Myth. "Fora." From Alcinoe. Aristotle gave her to a hag of Orlando the Furious.

Alcione Gr. Alcyone, daughter of Aeolus and wife of Ceyx, king of Trachis. She dreamed that her absent husband was shipwrecked, and in the morning she went to the beach where she found his dead body.

Alcira Ger. "The adornment of beauty." A Spanish city in the province of Valencia on the banks of the River Júcar.
Alci, Alzira

Alcmena Gr. "The one with the nasty temper." In Greek mythology, Alcmena was the wife of Amphitryon, whom Zeus seduced under the identity of her husband. Hercules' mother.

Alda Celt. "Beauty." Devoted Italian spiritual leader from Siena, famous for her visions of the life of Saint Salvador which are celebrated on April 26.

Aldana Sp. "The prettiest." Comb. form **Alda** and **Ana**.

Aldegunda Ger. "She who fights the nobility."
Adelgunda

Aldonza Ger. The old Spanish version of the feminine form of **Alfonzo.**

Alegra Lat. "Full of ardor." Daughter of Lord Byron. It means "happy" in Spanish.
Allegra, Allegria, Allegrita

Alejandra (fem. **Alejandro**) "Protector of men."
Alastrina, Alastriona, Alajandra, Alejandrina, Aleka, Alessanda, Alessandra, Alessandrina, Alessia, Alexa, Alexanderia, Alexandrina, Alexandrita, Alexena, Alexia, Alexina, Alexis, Ali, Alista, Alla, Alli, Anda, Elena, Lesy, Lexi, Sanda, Sandi, Sandra, Sandrina, Sasha, Sashenka, Sondra, Zandra, Zondra (Alexandra)

Alexia Gr. (fem. **Alexis**) "She who defends and protects." A bishop of Kiev in the 14th century.

Alfa Gr. Alpha, the first letter of the Greek alphabet. The name has almost a mystic quality, evoking the beginning of things. "I am the Alpha and the Omega," said God.
Alpha

Alfia Gr. (fem. **Alfio**) "One with white skin."

Alfonsa Gr. (fem. **Alfonso**) "Always prepared to fight." Argentine poet Alfonsina Storni.
Alfonsina

Alfreda OE. (fem. **Alfredo**) "Counsel from the elves." Mexican painter Frida Kahlo.
Alfi, Alfie, Alfita, Freda, Frida

Aliberta Ger. (fem. **Aliberto**) Var. **Alberto.** "Brilliant."
Berta, Bertita

Alicia Gr. (fem. **Alejo**) "The protector." Catholic saint whose feast is celebrated on June 15, also a character from the works of both Chaucer and Shakespeare. Derived from Adelaida, a princess.

Alida Ger. "Sublime." Form of **Adelaida** or new form of **Elida**.
Alidia, Élidia, Ali, Alidita

Alina Contraction of **Adelina**. Der. **Elina**.
Ali, Alinita

Alma Lat. "Kind and generous." The soul or spirit, biblical use.

Almira Arab. (fem. **Elsner**) "The princess." From Allah, all-powerful.
Almara, Almi, Almirita

Almudena Sp. "Our Lady of Almudena." The church named for her was the first Catholic church of Madrid. Name of the Virgin Mary in Madrid.
Alhóndiga, Almuda, Almudí, Almudín

Alta Lat. "Tall, strong-willed, and temperamental."

Altagracia "Our Lady of Altagracia" is used by some Dominican followers of the Virgin Mary who celebrate her feast on January 6.

Altair Arab. The brightest star in the constellation Aquila.
Alta, Altita, Altair, Águila

Alvina Ger. (fem. **Alvino**) "Friend of the elves."
Alvi, Alvita, Alvinita

Amada Lat. (fem. **Amado**) "Beloved." From the Greek Agapito or the Hebrew David.
Ama, Amadita, Amadora, Amato, Aimé, Doro

Amadís Lat. "The great love." Another form of Amada.
Amadisa

Amalia Ger. "Not troubled." Character in a romantic novel of the same name by the Argentine writer José Mármol (1817–71)
Amelia

Amancaí Quechua. In Argentina and Chile, *amancay* is a plant of yellow and orange flowers.
Amancay

Amanda Lat. (fem. **Amando**) Var. **Amado** "Beloved."

Amapola Arab. "Poppy flower."
Ama, Pola, Poli

Amaranta Gr. (fem. **Amaranto**) "Unfading glory."

Amarilis Gr. "Brilliant." Used frequently by writers during the Golden Age, also the name of a flower that often blooms at Christmas. It is similar to the Spanish word for yellow, *amarillo*.

Amarilla Gr. "The shiny one." "Yellow" in Spanish.

Amaru Peru. "Snake or boa" in Quechua, an Indian language.

Amata Lat. "Vestal Virgin." *Amor*, or Latin for "love."

Amatista Lat. "Amethyst." In Greek, "to fill with wine."
Ametista

Amaya Peru. "A beloved son" in Aymara, an Indian language.

Ambrosia Gr. (fem. **Ambrosio**) "Ever-living."

Amelia Ger. Var. **Amalia**. Protagonist of a novel of the same name by Henry Fielding, who presents her as the perfect incarnation of woman.
Amalia

América Ger. (fem. **Américo**) "The acting ruler."

Amiano Lat. From *amma*, the ancient child's word for "mama."

Amina Arab. (fem. **Amín**) "The faithful one." Mother of Muhammad.

Aminda Gr. "The protector." Protagonist of the *Fable Boschereccia* of Torquato Tasso.
Aminta

Aminta Gr. "The defender." In myth, Amintas was one of Narcissus's suitors. Aminta was also the name of three Macedonian kings.

Amira Arab. (fem. **Amir**) "The princess." Emir, name used by Spaniards to identify the descendants of Almanzor who founded small reigns called *Taifas,* when the caliphate of Córdoba fell.
Amiri

Amneris Lat. In Verdi's opera *Aida,* she is a rival for Radames's love.

Amona Lat. (fem. **Amón**) Amon, whose name signified occult and mystery, was the primary god of the Egyptians.
Ammoma, Amonía

Amonaria Gr. An Alexandrian virgin martyr whose name is a variation of **Amón** and **Amonía**.

Ampara Lat. "Favor and protection." The Virgin Mary was considered the "amparadora" of the Christians. Literally means "coat" or "covering."

Ana Heb. "Grace of God." From Hanna. Various biblical figures, including the mother of the Virgin Mary. Remembered July 26. Protagonist of the novel *Anna Karenina* by Leo Tolstoy (1828–1910).
Amamlas, Anabel, Anabela, Anabella, Anita, Aníbal, Anna, Anne

Anabela Comb form **Ana** and **Bella**. Subject of Edgar Allan Poe poem "Annabel Lee."
Anabella, Anabel, Anbel, Mabél

Anacaona "Flower of God." An indigenous (Taíno) princess from the island of Santo Domingo. She became queen of what is now called Haiti.
Anaca, Caona

Anacarsis Gr. One of Greece's legendary sages

whose name is derived from an ancient language now out of use.

Anacleta Gr. (fem. **Amacleto**) "Summoned." Derived from the Greek words that together mean to "call up." Anacletus, a saint of the first century.

Anadiomena Gr. "The emerging one." She who comes from the water. Surname of Venus, born from the blood of Caunos (who fell into the sea) in the coasts of Citerea.

Anahí Lat. Brazilian tree, called *ceiba* in Spanish (*Erythrina Crisa-galli*).

Anaio Phoenician. Divinity that reunited the attributes of Venus, Minerva, Ceres, and Diana.

Anais Fr. French author Anaïs Nin.

Analia Comb. form **Ana**, meaning "full of grace," and **Lia**, "the tired one."

Anastasia Gr. Various saints and martyrs of the church, including St. Anastasia, wife of the pagan Publius, mentioned in the Roman Canon. The church consecrates the second mass of Christmas to her.

Anatilde Comb. form **Ana** and **Matilde**.

Anatolia Gr. "The Oriental." From the Greek for "arise" and "complete," meaning "to make rise completely."

Andrea It. "The brave and elegant one." The Italian equivalent of *Andrés*, in Spanish it is the feminine version of that name.

Andrée, Andresa, Andreína

Andrómaca Gr. "The one who fights like a man." In Greek mythology, Andromache is the wife of Hector. Character of the tragedies of Euripides and Racine.

Andrómeda Gr. Offered as a sacrifice to a sea monster, Andromeda was saved by Perseus, who killed the creature.

Amedia "Repress modesty." Shamelessness and brazenness.

Anélida Comb. form **Ana** and **Elida**.

Anelina Comb. form **Ana** and **Elina**.

Anelisa Comb. form **Ana** and **Elisa**.

Anémona Gr. "Wind." The anemone, a type of flower that opens only when blown by the wind.

Ángela Lat. (fem. **Angel**) "Messenger." Christians believe the angels are pure of spirit and bring messages from God. Our Lady of Los Angeles. Her feast is celebrated January 27. Dominican singer Angela Carrasco.
Angeles, Ange, Angele, Angelina, Angelica, Angelita, Angefina, Angelines

Angélica Lat. "Like an angel." Heroine of the epic poem *Orlando Furioso* by Lodovico Ariosto. Mexican actress Angélica María. (See **Ángela**)

Angelina Lat. Dim. **Ángela**.

Angustias Lat. "Troubled by afflictions and anguish." In Spain, the Virgin of the *Angustias* is remembered September 15 and on Good Friday. Usually with María, as in María de las Angustias.

Ania Gr. "The afflicted." Religious martyr who lived in the third century, remembered August 13.
Aniana

Aníbal Phoenician. Var. **Hannibal,** from Hananbaal or Baalasin Bénéficant.
Annibale, Hannibal

Aniceta Gr. (fem. **Aniceto**) "Invincible." A pope and martyr from the second century.

Anisia Ger. (fem. **Anisio**) "Someone who keeps their word and finishes tasks." Saint and martyr, sacrificed by a soldier from the Emperor Galerio after confessing that she was a servant of Jesus Christ. Remembered on December 30.

Anita Heb. Dim. **Ana.** "Someone who is graced by God." Anita from *West Side Story*.

Annabel "Graceful and beautiful." Comb. form **Ana** and **Bella.**
Anabel, Anabella, Anabal, Annabal, Anna, Annabell, Annabella, Belinda

Annamaría Comb. form **Ana** and **María.** St. Anne and her daughter, the Virgin Mary.
Annamarie, Annemarie, Annmaria

Annelisa Comb. form **Anna** and **Lisa.**
Analisa, Analiese, Analise, Anelisa, Annelise, Annissa

Annette Fr. Dim. **Ana.**
Anett, Anetta

Annis Gr. Var. **Ana** or **Angela.**

Annora Lat. "Honor." Probably from Honora.
Anora, Anorah, Nora, Norah, Onora

Annunciata Lat. From the Annunciation, or the announcement that the Virgin Mary was to bear Jesus.
Anancinta, Anumziata

Anonna Lat. The Roman goddess of the annual harvest. Usually used for fall babies.

Anselma Ger. (fem. **Anselmo**) "She is protected by the gods."

Antía Gr. "Out front." Someone who is contrary or part of the opposition.
Anti, Antí

Antígona Gr. Antigone, daughter of Oedipus, who when he discovered he had committed incest and patricide, ripped his eyes out. Antigone became his gentle and faithful guide.
Antípates (Antigone)

Antíope Gr. Wooed by Jupiter, who changed his form to capture her. Their children were Amphion and Zethus.

Antonia Lat. (fem. **Antonio**) "Florid, rebellious."
Antoinette, Antoliana, Antolina, Antonette

Antonieta Lat. Var. **Antonia**. Marie Antoinette, queen of France, wife of Louis XVI.

Anunciación Lat. (See **Annunciata**)

Apia "Inclined to piety." Apphia, saint and martyr, disciple of St. Paul, remembered November 22.

Apancia Used in Mexico as the feminine of **Aparicio**, who introduced the cart to Spain.
Aparición

Apolinaria (fem. **Apolinario**) Apollonia, a virgin and martyr of the third century.

Apolonia Lat. (fem. **Apolonio** or **Apollo**) "Follower of Apollo."
Loni

Aquilina Lat. (fem. **Aquilino**) Related to *aquila*, "eagle."
Aquita, Aquilita, Lina

Arabela Lat. "Pretty altar." Cousin of James II of Scotland, who put her in prison for marrying William Seymour.

Araceli Lat. "Heaven's altar." *Ara* originally meant homebody, and *Celi* was from **Celeste**. The Roman St. Maria of Araceli had a sanctuary in the clouds near the temple of Jupiter.

Aracne Gr. Arachne, who represented with immense beauty in her embroideries the loves of Zeus and Europa.

Arcángela Gr. (fem. **Arcángel**) "Prince of angels."

Ares Gr. God of war.

Aretusa Myth. Arethusa, nymph that lived in a fountain in the island of Ortigia next to Syracuse.

Argentina Lat. (fem. **Argentino**) "Shiny like silver." The South American country.

Ariadna Gr. "A sweet and noble song, a breath of fresh air." Daughter of Minos and Pasiphae, who gives Theseus the thread by which he finds his way out of the labyrinth.

Aristófanes Gr. "Show yourself." Aristophanes, playwright (445–380 B.C.).

Arista

Armida Lat. "The light of power." The sorceress in Torquato Tasso's *Jerusalem Liberated*.

Arnalda Ger. (fem. **Arnoldo**)

Artemia Gr. (fem. **Artemio**) "Honest." Daughter of Dioclesis.

Artemisa Gr. (fem. **Artemio**) "Honest." Artemis, goddess of the hunt. Queen Artemesia II of Caria (fourth century B.C.), who built the Tomb of Mausolus in Halicarnassus for her husband.

Asela Lat. (fem. **Asellus**) Comes from the word for "burro" or "ass."

Aspasia Gr. "Welcomed." A friend of Pericles and also Aspasia of Phoenicia.

Asteria Lat. Taken from the Greek words for "shiny like a star."

Astidamia Gr. Daughter of Adminter, one of the wives of Hercules.

Astioque Gr. Astyoche, who gave birth to Hercules' son Tleptolemus.

Astria Norse. "Loved by the gods." Used sporadically by Hispanics who popularized the name of Astrid of Belgium, who died in 1935 in an automobile accident.

Astrea Gr. Astraea, daughter of Zeus and Themis, who visited the earth during the Golden Age.

Asunción Lat. "The highest point." Capital of Paraguay. The Ascension of the Virgin Mary is commemorated August 15.

Atabeira Mother of the supreme being in Haitian mythology.

Atalanta Gr. Mythological heroine and hunter.

Atanasia Gr. (fem. **Atanasio**) "Immortal." A saint, wife of St. Adrónico that the Ethiopian, Byzantine, and Coptic churches celebrate on December 9.

Até Gr. "The injustice." Personification of Delusion and goddess of rash actions, Ate was expelled from Olympus by Zeus.

Atergatis Syrian. In mythology, a creature with the body of a fish and the face of a woman.

Athena or Athana Gr. Athena, the warrior goddess, daughter of Zeus and Metis.
Thena, Thana, Thani

Athor Egypt. Goddess of beauty.

Ática Gr. (fem. **Ático**) "From Athens."

Atita From Atilla the Hun but also from the gothic **Alta** or "father" and *ita*, a diminutive, to make "little father."

Atocha From the Arab, Taucha or Atucho.

Audelina Ger. (fem. **Audelio**) "Famous prince."

Audrey OE. "Noble threat." One of the most popular saints from England, to whom many churches have been dedicated. Her feast is celebrated June 23.

Augusta Lat. (fem. **Augusto**) "Worthy of respect."

Áurea Lat. "Golden." This was the surname of Venus.

Aurelia Lat. "Gold." She sees and hears everything, even if it's on the sly.
Aranka, Auralin, Aurea, Aureliana, Aurita, Ora, Oralia, Orelia

Aureliana Lat. (fem. **Aureliano**) "Golden."
Auristela Lat. "Gold or golden star."
Aurora Lat. "Resplendent, brilliant." The Romans believed she was the goddess of dawn.
Ausca Pol. The Poles believe she is the goddess of the aurora.
Avelina Lat. (fem. **Avelino**) "From Avellino, Italy."
Avellana
Azael Var. Hazel.
Azalea Lat. From the flower azalea, but the Greeks relate it to something dry, arid, or without water.
Azucena Arab. Spanish for "lily."

B

Balbina Lat. (fem. **Balbino**) "Stutterer." Catholic saint remembered on March 31. From *balbus*, which gave us babble and other speech-related words that denote stammering.
Balbine

Baldomera Ger. (fem. **Baldomero**) "Brilliant or famous." St. Baldomero was a seventh century French hero who became a priest.

Baltilde or Batilde Ger. "Brave fighter." St. Bathild, queen of the Franks, wife of Clovis II remembered on January 26.

Bambi It. "Child." Dim. *bambino*. Also famous Walt Disney deer.
Bambina, Bambita

Bárbara Gr. "The foreigner." Very popular saint of the middle ages whose existence is doubtful, remembered on December 4. Originally, the Greeks called non-Greeks barbars or barbarians. Main character in *Doña Bárbara*, a novel by Venezuelan writer Rómulo Gallegos.
Bab, Baba, Babara, Babbie, Babe, Babette, Babita, Barbetta, Barette, Barbi, Barbra, Barbri, Barbrita, Barbro, Barby, Basha, Bobbi, Bonni, Bonnie, Bonny, Várvara, Varvita, Varina

Bartolomea Armenian. (fem. **Bartolomeo**) Virgin

saint who cofounded Sisters of Lovêre charity and died on July 26, 1833, at age twenty-six. Canonized in 1950.

Bartola, Barti, Bartita

Basha Pol. "A stranger." From the same root as Bárbara.

Basiana Lat. (fem. **Basiano**) "Sharp judgment." From the old Latin *bassus*, which means short or chubby.

Basilia Gr. (fem. **Basilio**) "Sovereign, King."

Basile, Basilie, Basilisa, Basille, Bazilia

Batilde Ger. "The fighter." From *badu* and *hild*, which both mean "fight."

Bathilda, Bazilia, Berthilda, Berthildre, Bertilda, Berilde

Baudilia Ger. (fem. **Baudilio**) "Brave."

Beatriz Lat. "Looks devout." Beatrice, favorite lover of Dante, who inspires the poems of the new life and whom he chooses as a guide in *The Divine Comedy*. Saint and martyr remembered on July 29.

Bea, Beata, Beate, Beatisa, Beatrice, Beatrix, Bebe, Beitris, Trixi, Trixie, Trixy

Beda Ger. "Insistent." English saint given the title of doctor of the church.

Begonia A flower discovered by a French botanist and named in honor of Bégon, an attendant of St. Dominic.

Begoña

Belarmina It. (fem. **Barlarmino**) "Beautiful armor."

Belén Spanish for Bethlehem, birthplace of Jesús, now in Israeli-occupied Jordan.

Belinda It. "Pretty, attractive." Catholic saint re-

membered on February 3. Probably from **Bella** and **Linda**.
Bel, Bella, Bellinda, Linda, Lindy

Belisa Lat. "The slender." Character in Lope de Vega's (1562–1635) comedy *The Sword of Madrid*.
Lisa

Belisaria Ger. (fem. **Belisario**) "The swordsman."

Benedicta Lat. (fem. **Benedicto**) "The blessed one."

Benigna Lat. (fem. **Benigno**) "Sweet." Character in Benito Pérez Galdós's (1843–1920) *Misericordia*.

Benita Sp. (fem. **Benito**) "Blessed." From the Latin Benedictus, name of many saints and therefore very popular.

Benjamina Heb. (fem. **Benjamín**) "Daughter." Derived from the words for son and right, as in the "good son."

Berenice Gr. "Leads to victory." Name of five Egyptian princesses and two Jewish ones. Queen of Judea in Jean Racine's Judaic tragedy. She follows Tito victorious to Rome.
Beranice, Bernice, Bernita, Veronica

Berlinda Ger. From *berin*, or "bear," and *lind*, or "sword."
Berengela, Bernalda, Bernilda

Berna Ger. (fem. **Berno**) "Rash."
Bernadeta, Bernadosa, Bernarda

Bernabela Aramaic. (fem. **Bernabé**) "Of the prophecy."

Bernarda Ger, (fem. **Bernardo**) "Like a bear." Bernadette, sainted little shepherd of Lourdes who had a vision of the Virgin Mary in the grotto of Massabielle. Remembered on April 16.

Berta Ger. "Brilliant, illustrious." Two saints, one

of them a martyr, remembered with Saint Rupert on May 15.

Bert, Bertalina, Berte, Bertha, Berti, Bertilia, Bertita

Bertilda Ger. "The illustrious combatant." Several saints bear this name in different forms.

Bertilia Ger. Two saints, Bertilia of Boscardín and of Mareuil, remembered on October 20 and January 3.

Betiana Ger. var. **Betina**. "Bright, shining."

Betsabé Heb. "Daughter of oath." Bathsheba, biblical figure, wife of Uriah, then David, and mother of Solomon.

Bersabea, Bátseba

Bety Heb. (dim. **Elizabeth**) "Pledged to God." Also used by English and Germans as a popular nickname for Elizabeth.

Betta, Betti, Bettie, Bettina, Betty

Bianca It. "White." The younger daughter in Shakespeare's *The Taming of the Shrew*. Nicaraguan Bianca Jagger, former wife of the Rolling Stones' Mick Jagger.

Blanca, Blancha, Blanchi

Biblis Lat. "Fountain." Saint martyr remembered on June 2. Mythological character, daughter of Mileta of Creta and of the nymph Idolea, that the water nymph turned into a fountain.

Blanca Ger. "White, fair." Heroine in Catalonian drama writer Ángel Guimera's (1847–1925) *Sea and Sky*.

Blanchi, Bianca, Blanquita

Blandina Lat. "The flattered one, the pleased one." Second century martyr, a slave girl who was killed by a bull.

Blanda, Blandine, Blandita

Blasa Gr. (fem. **Blas**) "Stammerer."

Bonifacia Lat. (fem. **Bonifacio**) "Does the right thing."
Bonita Sp. "The pretty one."
Boni, Bonnie, Bonny, Nita
Braulia Ger. (fem. **Braulio**) "Glows."
Brenda Ger. (fem. **Brendano**) Originally a Scottish name. The heroine of Walter Scott's 1821 novel *The Pirate*.
Brendita
Bricia Lat. (fem. **Bricio**) "Strong."
Brígida Irish. "The victorious." St. Brigid, abbess of Kildare, very popular and widely venerated in Ireland, celebrated on February 1.
Bridita, Brigidita
Britania Lat. "Britain." Britannia, the personification of the British Empire.
Brita, Britanita
Bruna It. (fem. **Bruno**) "Brown."
Brunella, Brunette, Brunetta
Brunilda Ger. "The warrior with courage." Brunhild, figure of Scandinavian and Germanic legend, popularized by Richard Wagner in The Ring Cycle of operas.
Bruni, Brunildita, Brunita, Nilda (Brunhilda)
Buena Sp. "Good."

C

Caledonia Lat. (fem. **Caledonio**) "From Caledonia." Caledonia is the Latin name for Scotland.
Callie, Cally

Cálida Sp. "Warm or tepid."

Camelia Flower brought from the Philippines by a German Jesuit named Kamel, who named the flower after himself. Heroine in Alexandre Dumas's *Camille*.
Camellia

Camila Lat. (fem. **Camilo**) "Novice to priesthood." Legendary figure, virgin, prototype of the warrior maiden that inspired Greek and Roman poems. Main character in late 1980's Argentine film *Camila*, based on the true story of a passionate romance between a priest and a parishioner in the late nineteenth century. It ends with their execution.
Cama, Camala, Camile, Camilla, Millie, Milly

Cancia Lat. (fem. **Cancio**) "From the noble Roman family of Ancios."
Canciana, Cancianila

Candelaria Lat. "The one who glitters, shines." Name often given to girls born the day of the Catholic celebration of the purification of the Virgin (February 2). Patron of Medellín. Usually

people march in the streets in Latin America with candles, or *candelas* on that day.
Candela, Candelas, Candelita, Candese, Candy

Cándida Lat. (fem. **Cándido**) "Incandescent." From the words meaning clear, immaculate, and shiny." Gabriel García Márques' *La cándida Erendira*.
Candi, Candita, Candy

Caridad Lat. "Theological virtue of love toward others." Black virgin, Nuestra Señora de la Caridad (Our Lady of Charity), a popular saint in Cuba, remembered on September 8.
Cari, Cary

Carina It. (fem. **Carino**) "Cute." Dim. **Caro**, which means "beloved." Italians use it as an expression of affection.
Cara, Cari, Cary, Karena, Karina

Carla Ger. (fem. **Carl**) "Strong." Dim. **Carolina**.
Carlita, Karila, Karla, Karlita

Carlina Der. Carlos. Var. Carolina.

Carlota Sp. (fem. **Carlos**) Puerto Rican clothes designer Carlota Alfaro.

Carmela Heb. "Garden." Biblical place name Mount Carmel, in Israel. Main character in Spanish movie *Ay, Carmela*.
Carmelina, Carmelita, Carmina, Lina, Lita, Mela, Melina, Melita, Mina

Carmen Lat. Var. **Carmelo**. Used in the past as a man's name also. Nuestra Señora del Carmen de Cuyo (Our Lady of Carmen from Cuyo) named general of the Andean army, is celebrated in Argentina on September 8. Character in Bizet's famous opera *Carmen* and in Prosper Mérimée's novel of the same name. Also actress, Carmen Miranda.

Carma, Carmelia, Carmelina, Carmelita, Carmencita, Carmina, Carmita, Karmen, Karmina, Lita, Mina

Carola Var. Carla. (Carol)

Carolina Lat. (fem. dim. **Carlos**) "Strong." Ger. Princess Caroline of Monaco. Venezuelan clothes designer Carolina Herrera.
Cara, Carla, Carlera, Carlina, Carlita, Carlota, Carol, Carolena, Carolinda, Cari, Carri, Carrie, Cary, Lina, Lola, Lolita

Casandra Gr. (fem. **Casandro**) "Brother of heroes." In mythology, Cassandra, daughter of King Priam of Troy, received from Apollo the gift of prophecy. Because she spurned Apollo's advances, he caused her prophecies to never be believed. In vain she warned the besieged Trojans against accepting the gift of a gigantic wooden horse presented by their Greek enemy; it was full of soldiers, who took the city captive.
Cassandra, Kasandera, Sande, Sandera, Sandi, Sandra, Sandy

Casia Lat. (fem. **Casio**) "The one who wears a helmet." Name of a noble Roman family.

Casiana Lat. (fem. **Casiano**) "Equitable, fair."

Casilda Ger. "The fighter." Saint and martyr, daughter of a Moorish king from Toledo, patroness of Burgos, city of Spain, remembered on April 9.

Casimira Pol. (fem. **Casimiro**) "Preacher of peace."

Casta Lat. (fem. **Casto**) "Pure."

Cástora Gk.(fem. **Castor**) "Brilliant."

Catalina Gr. "Pure, chaste." Various saints, among them Dominican Catalina of Siena of great sanctity and talent, remembered on April 30. Former U.S. Treasurer, Catalina Vásquez Villalpando. Katharina, main character in Shakespeare's *The*

Taming of the Shrew. Catherine, protagonist of Emily Brontë's (1818–1848) *Wuthering Heights.* Saint Catherine of Alexandria, martyr who was tortured on a spiked wheel. Empress Catherine the Great of Russia. Three of Henry VIII's six wives. The first was Catherine of Aragon (Catalina de Aragón)

Caren, Cari, Carin, Cassie, Catalín, Catarina, Cate, Cateline, Caterina, Catey, Cathaleen, Catheline, Catherina, Catherine, Cati, Catia, Catie, Catina, Catrin, Catrina, Katerina, Katina, Katrina, Trina

Cayetana Lat. (fem. **Cayetano**) "From Graeta, Italy."

Cecilia Lat. (fem. **Cecilio**) "Blind." From the Roman family of the same name. Roman martyr of the third century, patroness of musicians, remembered on November 22. Cuban novel *Cecilia Valdez.*

Ceceley, Cecely, Cecilí, Ceciliane, Cecilita, Celia, Cesia, Cilla, Cissie, Kikelia, Sacilia, Sasilia, Sesilia

Cefereina Lat. (fem. **Ceferino**) "Wind." Zephyr, a soft and soothing wind that signals the coming of spring.

Rina, Zeferina

Celerina Lat. "Quick." The Greek words for racehorse.

Celeste Lat. "Blue sky." Refering to the light blue color of the sky. Puerto Rican political figure Celeste Benítez.

Cela, Cele, Celesta

Celestina Lat. (fem. **Celestino**) "Matchmaker." La Celestina, main character of Fernando de Rojas's (1475–1541) *Tragicomedy of Calixto and Melibea.*

Celestina, Celia, Celina, Selestina, Tina

Celia Lat. (fem. **Celio**) "From the hills of Rome."

Saint, companion of St. Ursula, remembered on October 21. Famous Cuban salsa singer Celia Cruz.
Celi, Celita

Celina Gr. Var. **Celeste.** Saint mother of St. Remigius, remembered in France on January 13. Also a short version of **Celestina.**
Salinda, Selinda

Celinda Gr. Var. **Celeste.**
Saldinda

Celmira Arab. "The shining one."

Celoisa Gr. "Aflame."

Celsa Lat. (fem. **Celso**) "Elevated spiritually."

Cenobia Lat. (fem. **Cenobio**).

Cerelia Lat. "Relating to springtime."

Cesaria Lat. "Devoted to Caesar." Saint, abbess, virgin, remembered on January 12.

Cesarina Lat. (fem. **César**) "King."
Cesárea

Chanel Fr. Surname of fashion designer Coco Chanel. Popular in the 1980s.

Chiquita Sp. "Little one." Common nickname all through Latin America. Known in the U.S. for the Chiquita brand of banana.

Chloe Gr. "Young, green shoot."

Cintia Gr. "From Mount Cynthos." This name is tied to the origin of the goddess Artemis. Woman who Propercio loved and sang to; he called her Cynthia.
Cinda, Cindi, Cinthia, Ciny, Cyndia, Cynthia, Sindi, Syndy

Ciprina It. (fem. **Cipriano**) "From Cypress."
Cipriana, Ciperianna

Cira Gr. (fem. **Ciro**) "Sir."

Ciríaca Gr. (fem. **Ciríaco**) "Pertaining to God."

Cirila Gr. (fem. **Cirilo**) "Majestic."
Ciselia Lat. (fem. **Ciselio**) "From the sun."
Clara Gr. (fem. **Claro**) "Spiritually lucid." St. Clare, virgin founder of the order of the Poor Clares, remembered on August 11.
  Chiara, Clarabel, Clareata, Clareta, Clari, Claribel, Claribella, Clarice, Clarinda, Clarisa, Clarita, Clayrinda, Clerisa, Cliara, Clora, Clorinda, Klara, Klareta, Klarisa, Kliára
Clarisa Var. **Clara**. "Pertaining to the order of Clares." Clarissa, heroine of Samuel Richardson's (1689–1761) novel of the same name.
Claudia Lat. (fem. **Claudio**) Saint from the first century of Christianity, who was the mother of Pope Lino and Saint Ireneo, remembered on August 7.
  Claudeta, Claudina, Claudita
Claudina Lat. Variation of **Claudia**. Claudine, heroine of a series of novels by Colette, published under the pseudonym "Willy."
Clelia Gr. "The glorious." Ancient heroine in Roman history who was given as a hostage to the Etruscan King Porsena.
Clementina Lat. (fem. **Clemente**) "Compassionate." A Puritan name that suggested virtue. Subject of Stephen Foster's song *"My Darling Clementine."*
  Clementia, Clementine, Klementina
Cleofé (fem. **Cleofás**) "Vision of glory." María Cleofé, one of the three Marys who accompanied Jesus to Calvary.
  Cleofito, Cleo
Cleopatra Gr. "The glory of the father." Three queens of Egypt and one of Syria. Saint, martyr

remembered on October 19. Character in Shakespeare's *Antony and Cleopatra*.
Clea, Cleo, Clio

Clodomira GR. (fem. **Clodomiro**) "Captain of illustrious fame."
Clodi, Clodomita

Clorinda Lat. "Fresh, luxuriant." Character in Italian epic poet Torquato Tasso's (1544–95) *Jerusalem Liberated*.
Clora, Clori, Clorita

Cloris Var. **Clorinda**. In mythology, Chloris, queen of flowers, wife of Zephyr.

Clotilde Ger. "Illustrious warrior." Saint, queen of France, who converted her husband the King Clovis I to Christianity. Remembered on June 3.
Clodita, Clotilda, Klotilde

Coleta Fr. **Colette**, saint who reformed the Poor Clares order and founded the Coletinas branch, remembered on March 6.
Coleta, Coletita, Collet, Colleta, Colletta, Nicola, Nicoleta, Nicolletta

Colomba/Columba Lat. "Dove." Columbretes, islands off the coast of Valencia, Spain. Heroine in French novelist Prosper Mérimée's (1803–70) *Colomba*. Spanish saint Columba of Sens, remembered on December 31.
Collie, Colly, Colombia, Colombina, Colombita, Columbia, Columbias, Columbita

Concepción Lat. Through the Immaculate Conception, the Virgin Mary was born free of Original Sin.
Ceta, Chiquita, Chita, Ciquia, Concha, Concheta, Conchita

Constancia Lat. (fem. **Constancio**) "Firm."

Constan, Constancia, Constanta, Constantina, Constantita

Constantina Lat. (fem. **Constantino**) "Firm."

Consuelo Lat. "She who brings consolation during times of affliction and pain." Santa María del Consuelo in Spain, celebrated on June 21.
Chela, Consulata, Consuela, Consuelita

Cora Gr. "Young." In mythology, nickname for Proserpina, daughter of Ceres, kidnapped by Pluto.
Carina, Corabel, Corabelita, Corabella, Corena, Coreta, Corilla, Correna, Corrensa, Corresa, Corry, Karina, Kora, Korabel, Koreta, Korina

Coralia Gr. "Having the qualities of coral."
Cora, Coralí, Coralina, Coralinda, Coralita

Corazón Spanish word for "heart." Former Philippines president Corazón Aquino.

Cordelia Lat. "Little heart, as an expression of affection." The good daughter in Shakespeare's tragedy *King Lear*. She represents kindness in the midst of passions and the savage fury of the elements. Puerto Rican actress Cordelia González.
Cordela, Cordelita, Delia, Della, Kordelia

Corina Dim. Cora. Character in French writer Madame de Staël's (1766–1817) novel, *Corinne, or Italy*.
Carina, Carinna, Corena, Corín, Corina, Corita, Karina, Korina, Korinita

Cornelia Lat. (fem. **Cornelio**) "Like a horn." Comes from a famous Latin clan name and was often used during the Roman Empire.
Cornalia, Cornela, Cornelita, Cornelija, Kornela, Nelia

Corona Sp. "Crown." More used as the diminutive **Coronita** or "my little crown." Also the name of a very popular Mexican beer in the U.S.
Coroneta, Coronita

Crescencia Fr. (fem. **Cresencio**) "Related to the crescent moon."
Cresencita, Cresentia, Cresida
Crisanta Gr. (fem. **Crisanto**) "Goldflower."
Crispina Lat. (fem. **Crispín**) "Curly-haired." Crispina of Tagora, saint and martyr remembered as one of the most virtuous women in Africa, killed in Tereste on December 5, 304.
Cristina or Cristiana Lat. (fem. **Cristian**) "Of or relating to being a Christian." St. Cristina, patroness of Palermo, Italy, remembered on July 24. Talk show host Cristina Saralegui, Cuban writer Cristina García. Mexican-American writer María Cristina Mena.
Crista, Cristal, Cristi, Cristinita, Tina
Cruz Lat. "Cross." Catholics celebrate the sainted cross on December 14.
Custodia Lat. (fem. **Custodio**) "Guardian angel."

D

Dafne Gr. "Laurel tree." In mythology, Daphne was a nymph with whom Apollo fell in love. To free his daughter from Apollo's pursuit, Daphe's father turned her into a laurel tree.
Dafnita

Dagmar Ger. Unclear meaning.
Dagmarita, Dagmaris

Daira Gr. "Knowledgeable." Poetic character in Argentine writer Leopoldo Lugones's *La copa inhallable* (The Unfindable Glass).

Daisy OE. Popular nineteenth-century flower name adopted by many writers, including Henry James in *Daisy Miller*. MTV host Daisy Fuentes.

Dalia Lat. Like the flower of the same name, named after the Swedish botanist Andersdahl.
Dali, Dalila (Dahlia)

Dalila Heb. "Languishing." In the Bible, Delilah betrays Samson by cutting his hair, thus depriving him of his strength. Symbolizes the eternal feminine, with its enchantments and dangers.
Lila (Dalia)

Dalinda Gr. Var. **Delinda**. Der. **Delia**. One of the names of the goddess Diana.
Dalin

Dalmacia Lat. (fem. **Dalmacio**) "From Dalmatia."

Dalmira Ger. (fem. **Dalmiro**) "Illustrious."
Delmira

Damaris Gr. "Calf." In the New Testament a Damaris was converted by Saint Paul.
Damara, Mara, Mari

Daniela Heb. (fem. **Daniel**) "God is my judge." Mexican singer Daniela Romo.
Danela, Dani, Danice, Danila, Danita, Danitza (Danielle)

Danila (fem. **Danilo**)

Daría Gr. (fem. **Darío**) "Rich." Saint, martyr remembered on October 25.
Dari, Dariana, Darianna, Darice, Daricita (Daria)

Dativa Lat. (fem. **Datiro**) Saint, martyr remembered on December 6.

Davina Heb. (fem. **David**) "Loved one."
Daviana, Davinia, Davita, Devina, Divina, Divinia

Débora Heb. "Laborious like a bee." A prophetess, judge, and a military leader of Israel in the Old Testament. Puerto Rican Miss Universe Deborah Carthy.
Deb, Debbie, Debra, Debby, Debera, Devora, Devorah (Deborah)

Décima Lat. "Tenth."
Decia

Delfina Gr. (fem. **Delfino**) "Dolphin."

Delia Gr. "Born on the Island of Delos, Greece." One of the names of the goddess Diana. Cordelia González is a famed Puerto Rican actress. Carmen Delia DiPini, Argentine singer.
Delita, Lia

Delicia Lat. "The one who pleases."
Dee, Dela, Delia, Delise

Delta Gr. Fourth letter of the Greek alphabet.

Demetria Gr. (fem. **Demetrio**) Demeter, the mother goddess of the earth.
Demetra, Demetris
Deolinda Gr. (var. **Teodolinda**)
Desdémona Gr. "The unfortunate." In Shakespeare's *Othello*, she is the beautiful heroine wrongly accused of adultery by her husband who ends up murdering her and then committing suicide.
Desmona
Desideria Lat. (fem. **Desiderio**) "The desired one."
Desiré Fr. "Desired."
Desideria, Desi, Desirita (Desireé)
Devota Lat. "Devout, faithful, loyal to God." Patron saint of Monaco remembered on June 27.
Deyanira Gr. "Devastating." The name of Hercules' wife. Puerto Rican Miss Universe Dayanara Torres.
Dejanir
Diana Gr. "Divine." Roman goddess associated with hunting, chastity, and the moon. Very popular in Latin America. Religious woman remembered on June 9. Main character in English novelist and poet George Meredith's novel *Diana of the Crossways*. Lady Diana Spencer of England. Dianna (Diane)
Digna Lat. "Deserved, worthy." A Spanish saint martyred in Cordoba and remembered on June 14.
Dimas Gr. "Companion." In mythology, son of Algimios, who allied himself with the heraclids in their last expedition to the Peloponnisos peninsula in the south of Greece. Name the Greek church gave to the good thief crucified on the right side of Jesus. Remembered on March 25.

Dina Heb. "The judged one." In the Bible, daughter of Jacob and Leah.
Dinita (Dinah)

Dionisia Lat. (fem. **Dionisio** Var. **Denise**) "Devoted to Dioynsus." Saint Dionisia, remembered on December 6.

Divinia It. "Divine."

Dolores Lat. "Sorrows, pains." The Virgin Mary as the Virgin of the Seven Sorrows, remembered on September 15 or on Good Friday. Mexican actress Dolores del Río. Cuban-American playwright Dolores Prida.
Dela, Delores, Dolo, Lora, Loras

Domicana Lat. (fem. **Domicano**) Woman from the Dominican Republic.
Domi (Domingo)

Domicia Lat. (fem. **Domicio**) "Lover of home."

Dominga Lat. (fem. **Domingo**) "Devoted to God."

Dominica Lat. "Pertaining to the Order of the Dominicans." Two saint martyrs remembered on July 6 and February 5.

Domitila Lat. (Var. **Domicia**) St. Domitila converted her garden near Rome to a Christian cemetery that is known as the Catacombs of Domitila.

Donatila Lat. (fem. **Donato**) "Given." Used instead of Donata.

Donina Lat. "Gift, present."

Donosa Lat. "With grace, charm."

Dora Gr. "Gift." First wife of David Copperfield in Charles Dickens's (1812–70) novel *David Copperfield*.
Doralia, Doralyn, Dorelia, Dorena, Dori, Dorita

Doraluisa Comb. form **Dora** and **Luisa**.
Dora, Dorita, Lisa, Lista (Dora)

Dorcas Aramaic. Assimilated by the Greeks. "Gazelle." In the Bible, woman resuscitated by Saint Peter.

Dorelia Comb. form Dora and Aurelia. (Dora)

Dorinda Gr. Var. Dora.

Doris Gr. (fem. **Dorian**) "From Doris, an area in Greece." Mythological deity: wife of Nereus, mother of the Nereids, daughter of Oceanus. Actress Doris Day.

Dorotea Gr. (fem. **Doroteo**) "Gift of God."
  Dora, Dori, Dorinda, Doro, Doroteyo (Dorothy)

Drusila Lat. Feminine version of a Roman clan name frequently used in South America. **Drusela**

E

Edelmira Ger. (fem. **Edelmiro**) "Celebrated for nobility."

Edilia Gr. "Agreeable, sweet."

Edita Ger. "Rich, owner of possessions." St. Edith of Wilton, of whom people tell of various apparitions, remembered on September 16. (Edith)

Edith Heb. (maybe) In the Bible, wife of Lot who turns into a statue of salt for looking back on Sodom. Edith Piaf, famed French chanteuse.
Dita, Eda, Edi Edita

Edna Heb. "Enjoyment." Very popular because of its association with the biblical garden of Eden.
Ediva, Ednita, Edni

Eduarda Ger. (fem. **Eduardo**) "One who tends the land."

Eduvigis Ger. "Fortunate in battle." St. Eduvigis born in Bavaria, Germany, sister of Gertrudis—the mother of St. Isabel of Hungary—who became a nun in Trebnitz after becoming a widow. Included in the general calendar of the Western Church, celebrated on October 16.

Efigenia Gr. "Woman of strong race." In mythology, Iphigenia, daughter of Agamemnon.
Efi

Egda (fem. **Egdón**)

Egidia Gr. (fem. **Edigio**) "Natural of Egeo."

Egle Gr. "She who has brilliance and splendor." Aglaea, one of the three graces.

Elba Celt (probably) "She who stands out for her height." Scottish abbess of uncertain standing.
Elbita

Elcira Ger. "Noble adornment." Var. the ancient Alcira.

Elda Ger. "Fighter." Nuestra Señora de la Soledad de Elda (Our Lady of Solitude of Elda), venerated in Spain in the town of Elda in Alicante on December 11.
Eldi, Eldita

Elena Gr. "The glittering." In mythology, Helen, wife of Menelaus, whose kidnapping by Paris provoked the Trojan war. St. Helen, mother of Emperor Constantine the Great, remembered in the west on August 18. Mexican writer Elena Poniatowska.
Elaina, Elenita (Helen)

Eleodora Gr. (fem. **Eleodoro**) "Gift of the sun."

Eleonora Gr. Var. **Leonor**.

Eleuteria Gr. (fem. **Eleuterio**) Greek goddess of liberty.

Elga Slavic. "Sacred."
Helga

Eliana Lat. (fem. **Elian** or **Eliano**) "From the Roman family Aelia." Saint born in Amasea del Ponto, Italy, remembered on August 18.

Élida or Élide Gr. From the Elide valley, in the Peloponnesus region in Greece.

Elinda Var. **Belinda**.

Elisa Heb. "God is oath." Der. **Elizabeth**.

Elma Gr. (fem. **Erasmo**) "Amicable, desirable."

Elmira Arab. "Aristocratic lady."
Almeria, Almira

Elodia Ger. "The one who has all her wealth." Saint, martyr from Huesca, Spain, remembered on October 22.

Eloisa Fr. form of **Louise**. Héloïse, remembered for her love correspondence with the philosopher and theologian Abélard in the twelfth century.

Elsa Var. **Elisa**. Dim. **Elizabeth**. Incorporated by use to Spanish.
Elsie, Elsita, Ilsa

Elva It. Meaning unclear.

Elvira Ger. "Joyful and loyal." Four queens of Aragón and an Infanta in Spain. Saint, virgin, and martyr of Austria, remembered on January 25. Character in Spanish writer José de Espronceda's *The Student of Salamanca*.
Elvi, Elvirita

Ema Ger. "Gentle, brotherly." Austrian saint, countess, founder of the monastery of Gurk, remembered on June 29. Actress Emma Thompson.

Emérita Lat. (fem. **Emerito**) "A Latin soldier."

Emilia Lat. (fem. **Emilio**) From the name of a Roman family.
Emily, Emilita

Emperatriz Lat. "The sovereign." Title of the emperor's wife in Spanish. Legendary Catholic saint, remembered on September 6.
Empe

Encarnación Lat. The Incarnation, or the union of divine and human in Jesus Christ.
Encarna

Engracia Lat. "She who enjoys the friendship of God." Saint, martyr venerated in the diocese of Segovia, Spain, with her brothers Furtos and Valentín who lived in the Guadarrama Mountains in the seventh century, remembered on October 25.

Enid Welsh. "Life, spirit." Name from the legends of King Arthur.

Enriqueta Ger. (fem. **Enrique**) "Ruler of the land."
Enriquita

Epifanía Gr. (fem. **Epifanio**) "She who gives light." "Manifestation." The Epiphany feast remembering the three kings that visited baby Jesus the night he was born in Jerusalem.

Ercilia For some, "the refugee," from the Greek.

Erica Ger. (fem. **Erico**) "Honorable."
Enrica

Ermelinda or Hermelinda Ger. Comb. form of **Hermenia** and **Linda**.

Ermenilda Ger. "Powerful warrior."

Erminda Var. **Arminda**.

Ernestina Ger. (fem. **Ernesto**) "Severe or decisive."

Escolástica Lat. (fem. **Escolástico**) "Well-educated." Saint, sister of St. Benedict. Abbess of Monte Cassino, remembered on February 10.

Esmeralda Gr. "Pretty like the precious stone of the same name." Character in Victor Hugo's *The Hunchback of Notre Dame*.

Esperanza Lat. "She who trusts God." Spanish for "hope." Our Lady of La Esperanza, remembered on July 30.

Estela Lat. "Star." Var. of **Estrella**.
Este, Estelita, Estella

Ester Persian. "Star." In the Bible, main character in the book of Esther in the Old Testament, from which Racine took the plot for his renowned tragedy *Ester* (1689).
Estercita

Estrella Lat. "Star." Main character in *La Estrellita*

de Sevilla (*The Little Star of Seville*) which is attributed to Spanish writer Lope de Vega (1562–1635). The character is given the name Estrella because of her beauty and virtue. Also the name of a prominent Portuguese mountain range. Estrella Guitiérrez, an Argentine writer.
Estrelletta, Estrellita

Etel Ger. "Noble."

Etelvina Ger. "Noble friend."

Eudosia Gr. "Well thought of."

Eufemia Gr. "The one who says good words." Sixth century empress of the Orient.
Effi, Ufemia

Eugenia Ger. (fem. **Eugenio**) "Well-born." Saint, virgin from Spain who according to the legend, lived and dressed as a monk and was accused of a crime she could not have committed. Remembered on December 25.
Gena, Genia, Gina, Jenie

Eulalia Gr. "The one who speaks well." Spanish saint, virgin and martyr, Eulalia of Mérida, remembered in Spain on December 10. Spanish virgin and martyr copatroness of Barcelona, remembered on February 12.
Eula, Lalie

Eulogia Gr. (fem. **Eulogio**) "Good at reasoning."

Eusebia Gr. (fem. **of Eusebio**) "Pious."

Eustacia Lat. (fem. **of Eustacio**) "Giving fruit."

Eustaquia Gr. (fem. **Eustaquio**) "Tall."

Eva Heb. "The one who gives life." In the Bible, Eve, the first woman, wife of Adam who leads him to fall in sin. Argentinean Eva Perón.
(Eve)

Evangelina Gr. "The one who brings the good news." Heroine of Longfellow's narrative poem

Evangeline, A Tale of Acadie. Little Eva, female character in American writer Harriet Beecher Stowe's novel *Uncle Tom's Cabin.*
Eva, Evangelia, Evagelista

Evarista Gr. (fem. **Evaristo**) "Excellent."

Eveliana Lat. Var. Eva.
Evelia

Evelina Ger. or Fr. Possibly "hazelnut." Popular after Fanny Burney's novel, *Evelina.*

Everilda Ger. The one who fought the wild boar.

F

Fabia Lat. clan name. (fem. **Fabián**) Possibly meaning "one who grows beans."
Fabiana
Fabiola Lat. (Fem. dim. of **Fabio,** used instead of **Fabia**) Character in Cardinal Wiseman's novel of the same name. Fabiola de Mora y Aragón, queen of Belgium.
Fabricia Lat. (fem. **Fabricio**) "The artifice."
Fátima Unknown origin, probably Arab. Town of Portugal where three young shepherds witnessed an apparition of the Virgin that started the devotion for Our Lady of Fatima, remembered on May 13. Heroine in *A Thousand and One Nights*. Daughter of Muhammad, who married her cousin Ali and had three sons.
Faustina Lat. (fem. **Faustino**)
Fe Lat. "Faith." One of the three theological virtues, belief in the existence of and trust in God.
(Faith)
Febes Gr. "The splendorous." Saint discovered by St. Paul and remembered on September 3.
(Phoebe)
Federica Ger. (fem. **Federico**) "Peace lover."
Fedora Rus. (fem. **Fedor**) Gr. var. of **Teodora**. Her-

oine of French dramatist Victorien Sardou's *Fédora*.

Fedra Gr. (fem. **Fedro**) "Splendid." In mythology, Phaedra, daughter of Minos, king of Crete.

Felicia Lat. (fem. **Félix**) "Lucky."
Falicia, Feliz

Feliciana Lat. (fem. **Feliciano**) "Happy."

Felicidad Lat. "Satisfaction, pleasure, contentedness." Spanish for "happiness." Felisa. Puerto Rican politician Felisa Rincón de Gautier.

Felícitas Lat. Original Latin form of Spanish **Felicidad**. Felicitas, martyr, remembered on March 7. Felicity, martyr, mother of the second-century martyrs, the Seven Brothers.

Felipa Gr. (fem. **Felipe**) "Friend."

Fermina Lat. (fem. **Fermín**) "Constant, firm." Main character in French writer Valery Larbaud's *Fermina Márquez*.

Fernanda Ger. (fem. **Fernando**) "Courage."
Ferdinanda, Fernandina, Nanda

Fidelia Lat. (fem. **Fidel**) "Loyal."

Filipa Gr. "Lover of horses."
(Phillipa)

Filis Lat. "Leaves of the almond tree." In mythology, Phyllis, daughter of a king of Tracia who, after she thought her lover Demophon had left her, hanged herself and was transformed into an almond tree. Ideal transformation of the loved woman, cited by writers Ovid, Virgil, Horace, Garcilaso, Cervantes, and others.

Filomela Gr. "Lover of singing." Daughter of the King of Athens who metamorphosed into a nightingale.
Filomena

Fina Lat. "Of good figure and delicate manners." Also short for **Serafina, Delfina,** etc.
Finita
Fiorela It. (Dim. "flower," adapted to Spanish)
Flavia Lat. (fem. **Flavio**) An ancient Roman family.
Flaviana Lat. (fem. **Flaviano**)
Flor "Flower."
Flores, Florita
Flora Lat. "Gorgeous like a flower." In Roman mythology, goddess of flowers. Various saints. St. Flora, virgin and martyr of Córdoba, Spain, daughter of a Muslim and a Christian, remembered on November 24.
Floridita, Florita
Florencia Lat. (fem. **Florencio**) "Giver of flowers." Capital of Italy's Tuscany and used again to name towns in Argentina, Cuba, and Colombia.
(Florence)
Florentina Lat. (fem. **Florentina**) "From Florence."
Floriana Lat. (fem. **Florían**)
Florida Lat. "Flowery." Spanish conquistador Juan Ponce de León gave the name to the southern U.S. state for the many flowers he found there.
Florinda Var. **Flora.** Florinda Mesa, character in Mexican TV series *El chavo del ocho*.
Fortunata Lat. (fem. **Fortunato**) "Fortunate." Character in Spanish Benito Pérez Galdós's *Fortunata y Jacinta*.
Franca Ger. (fem. **Franco**) "From the Franks."
Francisca Ger. (fem. **Francisco**) "The one with the lance."
Francesca
Freya Slavic. "My lady." The Norse goddess of love, fertility, and death. Character in Bolivian writer Jaimes Freyre's *Castalia bárbara*.

Frida Ger. "The one who gives peace." Mexican painter Frida Kahlo (1910–54).
Fructuosa Lat. (fem. **Fructuoso**) "Fruitful."
Fulgencia Lat. (fem. **Fulgencio**) "Brilliant."
Fulvia Lat. "Reddish hair." Patrician Roman lady, wife of Marc Anthony who died when he left her for Cleopatra.

G

Gabriela Assyrian. (fem. **Gabriel**) "Heroine of God." Chilean poet Gabriela Mistral. Argentine tennis star Gabriela Sabatini.
Gaby

Gala or Galia Lat. (fem. **Galo**) "From Galia."

Gardenia Flower name, after eighteenth-century Scottish naturalist Alexander Garden.

Gema Lat. "Precious stone." St. Gemma Galgani (1878–1903) from Tuscany, Italy, remembered on May 14.

Genara Lat. (fem. **Genaro**) "Born in the first month."

Genciana Lat. (fem. **Genciano**) "Born blue."

Generosa Lat. (fem. **Generoso**) "Noble, generous." Saint, martyr of the church in Africa, who along with Esperanto and ten companions suffered martyrdom in the last year of the persecution of Marcus Aurelius, in the second century, remembered on July 17.

Genoveva Celt. "Of pale cheeks." Genevieve, patron saint of Paris, who according to tradition saved the city from the invasion of Attila, remembered on January 3. Genevieve of Brabante, a heroine of an old legend of the fifth or sixth century.
(Genevieve)

Georgina Gr. "From Georgia." Saint from Clermont of Auvergne, France, remembered on February 15.
Georginita

Geraldina Ger. (fem. **Geraldo**) "One who reigns with a lance." Incorporated into Spanish from French.

Gerarda Ger. (fem. **Gerardo**) "Strong with lance." Character in Spanish writer Lope de Vega's *La Dorotea*.

Germana Ger. (fem. **Germán**) "Warrior." French saint born in Pibrac near Toulouse, known for her wisdom and virtues, remembered on January 15.
(Germaine)

Gertrudis Ger. "The virgin of the lance." Two saints, Gertrude of Nivelles, abbess, and Gertrude the Great, remembered on March 17 and November 16 respectively. Cuban poet and writer Gertrudis Gómez de Avellaneda. Rebel sister in the novel and movie *Like Water for Chocolate*.
Gertina

Gervasia Gr. (fem. **Gervasio**) "Lance of power." Gervi

Gilda Eng. (fem. **Gildo**) "Gilded." Some say from **Ermenegilda**.
Gildi, Gildita

Gisela Prob. from Ger. "Arrow, lightning." Introduced to Spanish from French Giselle.
Gisele, Giselle, Gisella, Gizela, Gizella

Gladys Eng. "Happy, content." Introduced to Spanish from the English word "glad."

Glenda Welsh. (fem. Gaelic **Glen**) "Good and fair."

Gloria Lat. "Vision and possession of God in heaven." Invocation to God and the Virgin. American feminist Gloria Steinem. Cuban singer Gloria Estéfan. Mexican actress Gloria Marin.
Glori

Gloriana Comb. form **Gloria** and **Ana.**

Gracia Lat. "Grace, who possesses the friendship of God." Feast of the Visitation, remembered on July 2.
Engracia, Graciana, Graciela (Grace)

Gregoria Lat. (fem. **Gregorio**) "Alert."

Griselda Ger. "Elder heroine." Character in Boccaccio's *The Decameron*, the meek wife who submits to numerous trials devised by her husband.
Grisel, Selda, Zelda

Guadalupe Arab. "River or valley of the wolf." Very popular Virgin, patron saint of Mexico, who appeared to Juan Diego in 1531. Cuban singer La Lupe.
Lupe

Guida Ger. (fem. **Guido**) "The man of the forest."

Guillermina Ger. (fem. **Guillermo**) "Protector of the firm will." Queen Wilhelmina of the Netherlands, who abdicated in 1948.
Mina, Mini (Willemina)

H

Haidée Gr. "Modest." The name was derived from the verb "to caress." It was brought into popular use by Byron in his poem *Don Juan* and by Alexandre Dumas's *Count of Monte Cristo*.
Aidée, Idé, Idecita, Haydecita, (Haydee or Heidi)

Halimeda Gr. "Thoughts of the sea."
Haleta, Haliceta, Halicita, Meda, Medacita

Hannah Heb. "Grace." The mother of the prophet Samuel in the Old Testament.
Ana, Hana, Nan

Heladia Gr. "Was born or lived in Greece."
Eladia

Helena Gr. Var. **Elena** "Glittering."

Helga O.G. "Saintly." Var. **Olga**.

Helia Gr. "The sun." Var. **Elia**.

Heliana Lat. Var. **Eliana**. "A Roman family, Aelia."

Heloísa Fr. Var. **Eloísa** or **Luisa**.
(Heloise)

Herlinda Ger. From the words for "infantry" and "sword." Var. **Erlinda**. A Belgian abbess from the eighth century.
Hermelinda

Hermia Gr. (fem. **Hermes**) "Messenger." A name popularized by Shakespeare's character in *A Midsummer Night's Dream*.
Hermias, Hermila, Hermilda, Herminia

Hermosa Sp. "Beautiful."

Hersilia Lat. According to one version of the legend, wife of Romulus, the mythical founder of Rome.
Ersila, Ersilia, Hersila

Hilaria Lat. "Happy."
Ilaria (Hillary or Hilary)

Hilda Ger. "Battle woman."

Honorata Lat. "Honorable." Honorata, bishop of Padua.
Honora, Onorata (Honora)

Hortensia Lat. "The gardener." In honor of Hortense Le Paute, wife of a famous French watchmaker.
Ortensia (Hortense)

I

Ida Ger. A Catholic saint, Ida de Herzfeld, remembered September 4. Also a frequent name in Greek mythology.
Idalena, Idalia, Idalina, Idela, Idelta, Idolina
Ilda Ger. Var. **Hilda.** "Battle woman."
Ileana Ger. Var. **Elena.** "Glittering.
Ilona Ger. Var. **Elena.** "Glittering.
Iluminada Lat. "Lit." The Spanish word for "illuminated."
Imelda Ger. A very Catholic name most associated in recent times with former Philippines first lady Imelda Marcos.
Immaculada Sp. "Without stain." A reference to the Immaculate Conception.
Indiana Gr. (fem. **Indiano**) Refers either to the new *Indias*, meaning America, or India itself.
Inés Gr. "Pure or chaste." Often associated with Agnes.
Inesita, Inessa, Yaecita, Ynas, Yuez (Inez)
Inga Scan. In Norse mythology, a God of fertility and peace.
Inge, Ingrid
Inocencia Sp. "Innocence"
Inocenta, Inocentia
Irene Gr. "Peace."

Iris Lat. "Rain now." Goddess of the rainbow, messenger of the gods.

Irma O.G. "Force."
Erma, Irmina

Isabel Sp. Var. Elizabeth. Heb. "Devoted to God." Associated with *bella,* the Spanish word for "pretty." Isabel is the name of several queens. Isabel Allende. Isabel Presley.
Bella, Belita, Berlicia, Isa, Isabelita, Isabella, Izabel, Izabella

Isadora Lat. "Gift of Isis." Isis was an ancient Egyptian goddess. Modern dance pioneer and feminist Isadora Duncan.

Isolda Ger. "Iron-fisted ruler." Associated with Wagner's opera *Tristan and Isolde.*
Isolda, Isolita, Isolina (Isolde)

Ivonne Fr. Var. Yvonne. "Yew wood."

Ivana Heb. (fem. Ivan) "Jehova is gracious." Associated most recently with Ivana Trump.
Iva, Ivanna

J

Jacinta Gr. (fem. **Jacinto**) "Flower."
Jamila Arab. (fem. **Jamil**) "Beautiful."
Jaquelina Fr. (fem. **Jacques** Var. Jacob.)
(Jacqueline)
Jazmín Per. Name of a flower from India that is white and has a delicate perfume.
Jazmina, Yasmín, Yasmina (Jasmine)
Jenara Lat. (fem. **Jenaro**) "January."
Jenny Contraction of Johanna or a derivative of Jane. A completely English name.
Jessica Heb. "He sees." Daughter of Shylock in Shakespeare's *The Merchant of Venice*.
Jesusa Heb. (fem. **Jesús**) "The son of God."
Chucha, Chuyita, Gesuina
Jimenia Heb. (fem. **Jímeno**) Var. **Simeón**. "One who listens."
Jorgina Gr. (fem. **Jorge**) "Earth."
José In the past, commonly used as a woman's name followed by a female name, as in **José María**. Still used in Spain.
Josefa Heb. (fem. **José**) "God increases."
Chepa, Fefe, Josefina, Josette, Pepa, Pepita
Josefina Heb. (fem. **José**) "Jehovah increases." Empress Josephine, wife of Napoléon I.
Fefe, (Josephine)

Jovita Lat. (fem. **Jupiter**)
Juana Heb. (fem. **Juan**) "God is beneficent."
Juanita
Julia Lat. (fem. **Julio**) "Youthful.." Mexican poet Sor Juana Ines de la Cruz. Uruguayan poet Juana de Ibarburo. Puerto Rican poet JJulia de Burgos.
Juliaca, Juliana, Julieta, Julina, Julitta (Julie)

K

Karen A Danish form of **Catalina** used by Hispanics with an emphasis on the first syllable.
Carin, Carín, Caron, Carona, Kari, Karín (Karen, Kathy, Katherine)
Karina Lat. Var. **Cara.** "Dear one."
Karla Eng. Var. **Carla.** "Man."
Katerina Gr. Var. **Caterina.** "Pure."
Kati, Katy, Katrina (Katherine)
Kelila Heb. "Crowned."
Kayla, Kayle, Kyla
Kiana Modern variant of **Kita** and **Ana.**
Kita Sp. A slang translation of **Kitty.**
Kora Gr. "Maiden." Coined (as Cora) by American writer James Fenimore Cooper in *The Last of the Mohicans* (1826).
Cora, Corabel, Corabella, Cori, Korena, Korina

L

Lavinia Lat. In mythology, daughter of King Latinus, wife of Aeneas.

Lena Heb. An abbreviation of **Elena**.

Leona Gr. "Luscious."

Leonilda Ger. Comb. form **Leona** and **Nilda**.

Leonor Gr. "Light." Der. **Eleanor**.
  Lenora, Leona, Leonora, Leontina, Leopolda (Lenore)

Leopoldina Ger. (fem. **Leopoldo**) "Bold people."
  Leopolda

Lesbia Gr. It means "from the island of Lesbos, Greece" but is most associated with lesbianism. Used in Mexico.

Leta Lat. "Happy." St. Vincent's mother, who was martyred in Spain in the third century. Also an African bishop and a French hermit.
  Lelita

Leticia Lat. "Fertility." From the words that mean "to make the land fertile."
  Leti, Letizia, Letty, Tisha

Lía Heb. "Tired." In the Bible, Leah is Rachel's sister and Jacob's first wife.
  Liana (Leah)

Liana Fr. "To twine around." In Spanish the name of a vine common in tropical forests, such as the ones Tarzan used to move around.

Libia Gk. In mythology, Lybia was Poseidon's wife, who gave her name to North Africa.

Lidia Gr. "From Lidia." Lidia was a province of Asia Minor made famous by its two rich kings, Midas and Croesus.
Libia, Licia, Lida (Lydia)

Liduvina Ger. Formed by the words for "friend of the glorious people."
Lida, Lidy

Ligia Gr. "Melodius." The name of a mermaid and a character (Lygia) from the novel *Quo Vadis?* by Henryk Sienkiewicz (1896).

Lila Arab. "Night." Short for **Dalila.**

Lilia Gr. "Purity." The name of a Mediterranean flower that was later adapted by the English.
Lili, Liliana, Lilias, Liliosa, Lilla, Lilli, Lilly

Liliana Eng. Originally derived from **Elizabeth** or **Cecilia** with influence from the Latin *lirio.*
Lila, Lili, Lilia, Lilian, Liliana, Lilias, Lily (Lillian)

Lina Dim. **Adelina, Angelina, Carolina,** or **Magdalina.**
(Lena)

Linda Sp. "Pretty." (Dim. **Adelinda, Belinda, Gundelinda, Melinda, Regulinda, Siglinda, Teolinda,** which are mostly out of use.) Linda Ronstadt.
Lindi, Lindia, Lindita, Lindy, Lyn, Lynn

Linette Welsh. "Idol."
Linet, Lynett, Lynnette

Lita Dim. **Carmelita, Estelita, Isabelita,** and others with similar endings.

Lola Dim. **Dolores** or **Lorenza.**
Lola Flores, Lola Montez

Lolita Dim. **Lola.**

Lorena Fr. "From the Lorraine region of France."
Loren, Lorenita, Loreta, Lorneza (Lorenza)

Lourdes In 1858 Bernadetta Sourbiron saw the Virgin Mary in this section of France. Brazilians use Lourdette.
Lourdecita, Lourdetta, Lurdes

Lucelia A combination of **Luz** and **Celia**.

Lucía It. (fem. **Lucio**) "Light." Var. Lucy. Puerto Rican singer Lucecita.
Luci, Lu, Lucecita, Luciana, Lucilia, Lucina, Lucinda, Lucita, Lucza, Luz (Lucille)

Lucila Lat. (dim. **Lucia**) An Italian saint who died along with her father. California legislator Lucille Roybal. Actress Lucille Ball.
Luci, Lucia, Lucilla, Lucille, Lucina (Lucille)

Lucinda A poetic variation of **Lucina**, associated with **Clorinda** or **Belinda**.

Lucrecia Lat. Lucretia was a Roman matron who committed suicide because she was ashamed of being raped.
Lucrezia (Lucretia)

Luisa O.G. (fem. **Luis**) "Warrior." A French form of Ludwig.
Aloisa, Aluisa, Eloisa, Eloise, Heloisa, Lois, Lola, Lolita, Louisa, Loyisa, Lu, Ludorika, Ludovila, Ludwiga, Luise, Luisetta, Luisianna, Luisina, Luiza, Lujza, Lula, Lulita, Lúlu

Lula Dim. Luisa.

Luminosa Lat. "Gives light." A means of illuminating or giving life its light.

Luna Lat. "Moon."

Lupe (dim. **Guadalupe**) Used in reference to the virgin of Guadalupe who miraculously appeared

to a boy in Guadalupe, Mexico. Cuban singer La Lupe.
Lupita, Pita
Luz Lat. "Light." It recalls the Virgin Mary because it refers to bringing light.
Lydia Var. Lidia.

M

Mabel Eng. "Worthy of love." From Latin *amable*.
Amabel, Amable
Maciel Lat. "Skinny."
Madona Lat. "Lady." Often used to refer to the Virgin Mary. Singer Madonna.
Mafalda Ger. Lat. Var. **Matilde**. Saint, daughter of King Sancho I of Portugal remembered on May 2. Main character in famous Argentine comic strip *Mafalda*.
Magda Ger. Var. **Magdalena**.
Maida
Magdalena Gr. From Magdala, a town on the Sea of Galilee. St. Mary Magdalene, sister of Lazarus, sinner pardoned by Jesus, who was present at his crucifixion. Remembered on July 22.
Lena, Mada, Madalena, Madel, Magda, Magdala, Malena, Malina, Marlena, Marlene (Madeleine)
Maida Eng. "Maiden."
Magda, Maidel, Mayda, Maydena
Maité Basque. "I love you." Sometimes used as short for **María Teresa**.
Malena Short for **Magdalena**. Comb. form **María** and **Elena**.
Malva Gr. "Delicate." Also the name of a flower.
Melva, Melvina

Malvina Ger. "Friend of justice."
Mal, Malva, Mel, Melva, Melvina

Mamerta Lat. (fem. **Mamerto**) "From Momertium, Italy."

Manón Fr. Dim. **María**. Heroine in Abbé Prévost's *Manon Lescaut* (1731).

Manvela Heb. (fem. **Manuel**) "God is with us."
Manuelita

Marcela Lat. (fem. **Marcelo**) Sainted widow Marcella, named by St. Jerome "Glory of the Roman Matrons." Remembered on January 31.
Marcie, Marcy, Marquita (Marcella)

Marcelina Lat. (fem. **Marcelino**) Saint, virgin, sister of St. Ambrosia, remembered on July 17.

Marcia Lat. (fem. **Marcio**) "Born in March."
Marcelia, Marcina, Marcita, Marcy, Marquita, Martia

Marcolina Lat. (fem. **Marcos** and **Marcolino**) Probably "to break."

Mare Ir. Var. **María**.

Marena Comb. form **María** and **Arena**.

Margarita Gr. "Pearl." Various saints, among them St. Margaret, queen of Scotland, and St. Mary Margaret, princess of Hungary remembered on June 10 and January 26, respectively. Marguerite Gauthier, heroine of Alexandre Dumas's *Camille*.
Greta, Maggie, Maggy, Maiga, Marga, Margareta, Margerita, Margie, Margo, Margot, Marguarita, Marguita, Margy, Meta, Peggie, Rita

Margo Fr. Dim. **Margarita**.

María Heb. "Lady, chosen, exalted, love of God." Mother of Jesus, daughter of St. Joachim and St. Anne, wife of Joseph. Worshiped with a cult superior to any angel or saint. Main celebrations in her honor are on March 25, May 24, August 18, September 8, September 12, and December 8.

Also various saints and martyrs. This name has numerous variants as a result of its popularity. In the modern era it is frequently combined with other names. Ironically, not very common among young children today. TV journalists Maria Shriver and María Elena Salazar. Cuban actress María Conchita Alonso. Mexican actress María Félix. Main character in *West Side Story*. Main character in Colombian Jorge Isaacs's novel *María*.

Manon, Mara, Marabel, Mare, Mariam, Marian, Mariana, Maribel, Marie, Mariel, Mariela, Marilyn, Marion, Mariquita, Marita, Maritsa, Maritza, Marla, Maruga, Marya, Maura, Maurita, Miriam, Moya, Muriel (Mary)

Mariana Lat. (fem. **Mariano**) "Devoted to the Virgin." Comb. form **María** and **Ana**. Mariana de Jesús de Paredes y Flores, known as the Lily of Quito (Ecuador), remembered on June 2.

Mare, Marianita (Marian)

Marianela Lat. Comb. form **Mariana** and **Estela**. Main character in *Marianela*, Benito Pérez Galdós's novel of the same name.

Maribel Contraction of **María** and the French *belle*, "beautiful."

Maribella

Mariel Var. of **Mary**.

Mariela, Mariele

Marilú Comb. form **María** and **Luz**.

Mariliz

Marina Lat. (fem. **Marino**) "From the sea." Saint and martyr of Galicia, remembered July 18. Marina or Malincha, a Mexican-Indian woman married to Hermán Cortez.

Marena, Mariana

Marinés Comb. form **María** and **Inés**.

Marisol Comb. form **María** and *sol*, Spanish for "sun." First Puerto Rican Miss Universe Marisol Malaret.

Marité Comb. form **María** and **Ester**, also **María** and **Teresa**.

Marquesa Lat. (fem. **Marcos**) "to break."

Marta Heb. "Owner, lady of the home." Various saints and martyrs, among them St. Martha sister of Lazarus and Mary Magdalene, remembered on July 29. Main character in Catalan writer Angel Guinerá's *Tierra Baja* (Lowland). Argentine singer María Marta Serralina.

Martel, Martina, Martita (Martha)

Martina Lat. (fem. **Martín** and **Martino**) "Born on Tuesday." Seventh century empress, wife of Heradio. Martyr remembered on January 30. Tennis star Martina Navratilova.

Marti, Martimana, Tina

Matilde Ger. "Strong in war." St. Matilde, empress of Germany in the tenth century, remembered on November 16. Important female character in Stendhal's *The Red and the Black*.

Mati, Matilda, Tilda, Tilde

Maura Lat. (fem. **Mauro**) Var. Mary. "Of brown skin."

Mora

Mauricia Lat. (fem. **Mauricio**) Var. **Mauro**.

Maximiana Lat. (fem. **Maximiano**)

Máxima Lat. (fem. **Máximo**) "The greatest."

Maximina Lat. (fem. **Maximino**)

Maya Gr. "Mother." In mythology, daughter of Atlas and mother of Hermes, called by the Roman pagans "the good goddess." Indian empire that ruled the area that is today Mexico, Guatemala, and most of Central America.

Melania Lat. (fem. **Melanio**) "Dark-skinned." St. Melania, the young founder of a convent in Jerusalem, remembered on December 31.
Mel, Mela, Melani, Milena (Melane)

Mélida Lat. "Sweet like honey."

Melinda Gr. "Who sings harmoniously."
Linda, Malina, Malinda, Melina

Melisa Gr. "Bee." First woman Cretan priest, whose body was transformed into a bee for having wanted to divulge the mysteries of Demeter's cult.
Lisa, Malisa, Melita, Melosa, Mili, Millie (Melissa)

Mercedes Lat. "Gracious gifts or benefits." Refers to Santa María de las Mercedes, or Our Lady of Mercies, remembered on September 24. Argentine singer Mercedes Sosa.
Merce, Meche, Mercedita, Mercy

Micaela Heb. (fem. **Miguel**, instead of the rare **Miguela**) "Godlike."
Miguela, Miguelina, Miguelita
(Michaela)

Micol Heb. "Queen." In the Bible, Michal, daughter of Saul and wife of David.
Milca

Milagros Lat. "Miracles." The Virgin as Our Lady of Miracles, remembered on November 27. In Salta, Argentina, where the same virgin is venerated under the name Virgin of Miracle, the feast is celebrated on September 13.
Mila, Milagritos, Milagrosa

Milba Ger. "Amiable protector." Short for Milburga.

Mildreda Ger. "Soft-spoken, amiable."
Mildred

Mimi Dim. **María, Miriam.** Tragic heroine in Puccini's famous opera *La Bohème*.

Minerva Lat. Roman goddess of wisdom.
Min, Minetta

Miranda Lat. "Marvelous." Daughter of magician Prospero in Shakespeare's *The Tempest*.
Mira, Randa, Randi

Mireya "The admired one." Main character in Nobel Prize–winner Federico Mistral's poem of the same name.
Mía

Miriam Heb. Possibly "bitter" or "rebellious."
Mariam, Mimi

Mirna Gr. "Soft like perfume." Puerto Rican painter Mirna Báez.
(Myrna)

Mirta Gr. "Crown of thorns." Promoter of beauty products Mirta de Perales.

Modesta Lat. (fem. **Modesto**) "Modest."

Mona Ir. Gael. "Aristocratic." Island off the shore of Puerto Rico.

Mónica Gr. "Who lives in loneliness." Mother of St. Augustine, remembered on May 4. Tennis player Monica Seles.
Mona, Monique

Munira Arab. "Source of light."

N

Nadia Rus. "Hope." Gymnast Nadia Comaneci.
Nadina, Nadira

Nancy Eng. Dim. of **Anna** or **Hannah.**

Natalia Var. **Natal** or **Natalio** that was used widely in Russia as a diminutive of Natascha.
Natalina, Natasha, Natividad, Nattie

Natana Heb. (fem. **Natán**) "Given." Protagonist of *Blanquerna*, a novel by Raimund Lulio (1235–1315).

Natividad Lat. "Birth." Name given to children born September 8, the feast of the birth of the Virgin Mary.

Nelly Var. **Elena, Eleonora,** or **Cornelia.** Puerto Rican State Senator Nellie Santiago.

Nereida Gr. "Daughter of Nero." The Nereids, sea deities, daughters of Nereus and Doris.
Nerida, Neria, Nerina

Nicolasa Gr. (fem. **Nicolás**) "Leader in victory." Puerto Rican writer Nicholassa Mohr.

Nidia Gr. "She possesses sweetness and grace." U.S. Representative Nydia Velázquez.
Nydia

Nilda Var. **Brunilda, Leonilda,** and others.
Nylda

Nina Sp. Similar to *niña* or "girl." The *Niña*, one of Christopher Columbus's three ships.

Nita Sp. Dim. **Anita.**

Ninfa "Adolescent." Nymphs, mythological divinities that inhabit the forests.

Noemi Heb. "My grace, my glory." In the Bible, Naomi, the mother-in-law of Ruth.
(Neomi)

Norma Ger. "Normal." A protagonist from the Bellini opera of the same name.

Nubia Lat. From Nubia, region and ancient kingdom in northeast Africa.

O

Octavia Lat. (fem. **Octavio**) "Eighth." Augustus's sister, wife of Marc Anthony before Cleopatra.
Otavia, Tavia

Ofelia Gr. "The one who aids." Ophelia is the young woman in Shakespeare's *Hamlet* who goes mad. Puerto Rican actress Ofelia González.
Filia (Ophelia)

Olga Slavic. "The sublime, saint." Saint, wife of Prince Igor of Kiev, who with her grandchild St. Vladimir is venerated as one of the first fruits of Christianity in Russia. One of the sisters in Anton Chekhov's drama *The Three Sisters*. Cuban singer Olga Guillot.
Elga, Helga, Olguita

Oliana Polynesian. "Oleander."

Olimpia Gr. (fem. **Olimpio**) Olympias, mother of Alexander the Great.

Olinda Prob. from Gr. (fem. **Olindo**) "Scented."

Olivia Lat. "From Olivia, Italy." Martyr from Palermo, Italy, remembered on June 10.
Livia, Oliva, Olva

Oneida Am. Indian. "Long-awaited." Familiar in the U.S. as a brand of silverware.
Onida

Oria Lat. Vulgar form of Aúrea. Very popular saint

in Spain, nun in the Convent of Saint Millán of Cogolla, remembered on March 11.

Oriana Comb. form **Oria** and **Ana**. Main character in Garci Rodríguez de Montalvo's adventure novel *Amadis of Gaul*. Italian journalist Oriana Falacci.

Orquídea Lat. "Orchid."

Otilia Chile. Saint of Alsace who was blind until she was twelve years old and recovered her sight when she was baptized by St. Erhardo, remembered on December 13.
Odilia

P

Paca Sp. from Ger. (fem. **Paco**) "One with the lance."
Paquita

Paladia Lat. (fem. **Paladio**) "Protected by the goddess Pallas Athena."

Palmira Lat. From Palmyra, ancient city of Syria. Allusion to Palm Sunday, which marks the triumphant entrance of Jesus in Jerusalem.
Palma, Palmer

Paloma Lat. "Tame like a dove." Designer Paloma Picasso, daughter of the artist. Mexican singer Paloma San Bisilio.

Pamela Gr. "Who uses a straw hat, with low crown and wide brim."
Mela, Pam, Pamelia, Pamelina, Pamelita, Pami

Pandora Gr. "The one with all the attributes." In mythology, first woman on earth endowed with gifts from all the gods. Spanish group Pandora.

Parmenia Gr. (fem. **Parmenio**) "Studious."

Pascua Heb. "Sacrifice for the immunity of the people." Among the Hebrews, celebration of the abolition of slavery in Egypt. In Christianity, Resurrection Day. The Spanish word for Easter.

Pascualina Lat. (fem. **Pascual** and **Pascualino**) "Easter."

Patricia Lat. (fem. **Patricio**) "Of noble race." Saint pertaining to the imperial sixteenth-century Constantinople family.
Patti

Paula Lat. (fem. **Pablo**) "Short." Various saints, martyrs, and lay sisters, among them, St. Paula, widow who collaborated with St. Jerome in his biblical works, remembered on January 26.
Paola, Paulina, Paulita

Paulina Lat. (fem. **Paulino**) "Devoted to Paul."
Paulín

Paz Lat. "Peace." Devotion to Our Lady of Peace, originated in Toledo, Spain. Patron of El Salvador, remembered on January 24.

Penélope Gr. "Bobbin worker." In Greek mythology, Penelope, wife of Odysseus who put off the many suitors who courted her when it seemed that the wandering Odysseus must be dead, by telling them she couldn't marry until she finished the tapestry she was weaving. She would work all day and unravel her work at night, hoping that her husband would come home.
Pen, Penelopa, Peni

Pepita (fem. **Pepe**)
Pepa, Peta

Perfecta Lat. (fem. **Perfecto**) "Perfect, flawless." Main character in Benito Pérez Galdós's *Doña Perfecta*.

Perla Lat. "Person with excellent jewelry."
Perl (Pearl)

Petra Lat. (fem. **Pedro**) "Stone of the church." Short for **Petrona**.
Peitra, Peta, Petronela

Petrona (fem. **Petronio**)
Petronila

Petunia Trumpet-shaped flower with white and bright pink blossoms.

Pia Gr. (fem. **Pío**) "Pious."

Piedad Lat. "Piety, devotion." Virtue that inspires tender devotion for saintly things and compassion to fellow humans. Our Lady of Piety, remembered on August 15.

Pilar Lat. "Pillar." Our Lady of Pilar from Zaragoza, Spain, after an apparition on top of a pillar in the town, remembered on October 12. Allusion to the Virgin Mary in her role as "pillar" of the church.

Plácida Gr. (fem. **Plácido**) "Calm, tranquil."
Placidia

Porcia Lat. (fem. **Porcio**) "Roman lady." Portia is a character in Shakespeare's *Julius Caesar* and a heroine in his *The Merchant of Venice*.
(Portia)

Primavera "Spring."
Prima

Primitiva Lat. (fem. **Primitivo**) "The first one."
Primi

Primorosa Eng. "First rose." Nineteenth-century flower name.
(Primrose)

Priscila Lat. "From another epoch." A New Testament name revived by the Puritans.
Cilla, Pris, Prisca, Priscella, Prisilla, Prissy (Priscilla)

Prudencia Lat. (fem. **Prudencio**) "He who labors with sensitivity and reserve."
(Prudence)

Pura Lat. "Pure." Relating to the Virgin Mary, who is known as the purest of all women.

Q

Quintina Lat. (fem. **Quintin**) "The fifth."
Quirina Lat. (fem. **Quirino**) Relating to Mars, the god of war.

R

Rafaela Heb. (fem. **Rafael**) "God heals."

Rainelda Ger. "War of advisors." St. Rainelda, virgin, French martyr.
Raina, Raine

Ramona (fem. **Ramón**)

Raquel Heb. "Friend of God or Lamb of God." In the Bible, Rachel, Jacob's wife and Joseph's mother.
(Raquel or Rachel)

Rebecca Heb. "My secret is God." In the Old Testament, she was Isaac's wife.
Becky

Refugio Lat. "Refuge." In Mexico, the nickname is Luca.
(Refuge)

Regina Lat. "The celestial princess." St. Regina, virgin and martyr of the third century.

Reginaldo Ger. "Governs by the will of God."
(Reginald)

Reina Lat. Spanish for "queen." The Virgin Mary was referred to as the queen of the apostles.

Reinalda O.E. (fem. **Reinaldo** Var. Reginald.) "Counsel power."
Reinelda, Reineldis, Rieneria

Renata Lat. (fem. **Renato**) "Born again."

René Fr. A French form of **Renata.**
Rita Dim. **Margarita.** St. Rita of Cascia, patron of desperate cases, remembered May 22.
Rosa Lat. The flower, rose, whose name was adopted by St. Rosa of Viterbo in France and most significantly by St. Rose of Lima, Peru. Actress Rosie Peréz. Civil rights activist Rosa Parks. German socialist leader Rosa de Luxemburg. Rosalba, Rosalía, Rosalin, Rosalina, Rosalinda, Rosamaria, Rosana, Rosaria, Rosario, Rosaura, Rose, Roselina, Rosella, Rosemarie, Rosemary, Rosemunda, Rosita, Rósula, Rosundo, Roxana (Rose)

S

Sabina Lat. (fem. **Sabino**) "From Sabino." Saint martyred by orders of Emperor Adrian, remembered on August 29.

Sabrina Lat. "From the area of the Severn River in Great Britain."

Safo Gr. "The one who sees with clarity." Sappho, sixth-century B.C. Greek lyric poet born on the island of Lesbos. Main character in Honoré de Balzac's novel of the same name.
(Sappho)

Salomé Heb. (fem. **Salomón**) "One who loves peace." In the gospel, Mary Salomé, mother of John the Evangelist and James the elder.
Sally

Salvadora Lat. (fem. **Salvador**) "Savior." Name given to the Virgin Mary for having saved humanity, remembered on July 20 at the sanctuary of Superga in Turin, Italy.

Salvia Lat. "Saved, with reference to health."

Sandra It. Short for **Alessandra**. Mexican-American poet Sandra Cisneros.
Sandie, Sandrita, Sandy, Sondra, Zandra

Santina Lat. (fem. **Santos**) "Saint." Dim. **Santa.**

Sara Heb. "The princess." In the Bible, Sarah was

the wife of Abraham and the mother of Isaac. St. Sara of Sceré, Egypt, remembered on July 13.
Chiquita, Sarah, Sarita, Sasha, Zara, Zarela

Saula Gr. (fem. **Saulo**) "Tender, delicate."

Segunda Lat. (fem. **Segundo**) "Second." Two Italian martyrs, one known as St. Rufina, the other as St. Esperato.

Selina Gr. "Moon goddess." Most recently associated with Selina Quintanilla, the Tejano musician killed in Texas the same year she won a Grammy Award.

Selma Probably from Arab. "She who has peace." For some, short for **Anselma**.

Serafina Heb. (fem. **Serafín**) "Angels with wings."

Servia Lat. (fem. **Servio**) "Child of slaves."

Severino Lat. (fem. **Severino**) "Firm with justice."

Sidonia Lat. (fem. **Sidonio**) "From Sidon, France."

Sila Heb. Var. **Zilla**. "Shadow."

Silvana (Lat. fem. **Silvano**) "One who lives in the forest."

Silveria Lat. (fem. **Silverio**) "Born in the forest."

Silvia Lat. (fem. **Silvio**) "Of the forest." In Roman mythology, Rhea Silvia, mother of Romulus and Remus, founders of the Eternal City. Mexican actress Silvia Pinal.

Silvina Lat. (fem. **Silvino**)

Sinforosa Gr. (fem. **Sinforoso**) "One with many talents." Saint martyr of Tivoli, Italy, with her seven children, remembered on July 2.

Sira Lat. (fem. **Siro**) "From Syria."

Siria Per. "Brilliant like the sun." Syrus, mythological divinity, credited with invention of arithmetic. Syria, country in western Asia.
(Syria)

Siseta Lat. "Native of Sis, Armenia." Character in

Benito Pérez Galdós's *National Episodes*, particularly in the one referring to Cádiz.

Sixta Lat. (fem. **Sixto**) "Courteous and refined."

Socorro Lat. "The one who gives help and protection." Spanish for "aid, help." Nuestra Señora del Perpetuo Socorro (Our Lady of Perpetual Help), remembered on the third Sunday of June.

Sofía Gr. "The one who possesses wisdom." A regent of Russia and a regent of England. Queen Sofia, present monarch of Spain. Greek saint, martyr whose name was given to the temple that Constantine built in Constantinople and that the Muslims converted to a mosque, remembered on August 1. Actress Sophia Loren.

Sol Lat. "Of luminous faith." Spanish for "sun." Doña Sol, character in Vicente Blasco Ibáñez's *Sangre y arena* (*Blood and Sand*).

Soledad Lat. "Left alone." Nuestra Señora de Soledad (Our Lady of Solitude), who evokes the moment when Jesus died, remembered on Friday and Saturday of Holy Week. Singer Soledad Bravo.

Sonia Rus. Slavic diminutive of **Sofía**. Sonya, character in Fyodor Dostoyevski's *Crime and Punishment*. Brazilian actress Sonia Braga

Stella Maris Lat. "Star of the sea."

Susana Heb. "Pure woman." In the gospels, a devout Jewish woman who was falsely accused of adultery by two old men but saved from execution by Daniel.

Susan, Susannah, Susi, Suzi

T

Tamar Heb. A biblical figure who was David's daughter and Absalom's sister.
Tamar, Tamara, Tammy

Tatiana Lat. A latinization of the Greek *taciana*. Heroine of the novel *Eugenio Onequín* by Alexander Pushkin.

Telma Heb. (fem. **Telmo**)
(Thelma)

Teodora Gr. (fem. **Teodoro**) "Son of God." St. Teodora of Alexandria, remembered September 11.

Teodosia Gr. (fem. **Teodosio**) "He gives to God." St. Teodosia, martyr of Palestine and the virgin of Constantinople, remembered April 2 and May 29.

Teresa Gr. "The hunter." Various saints and martyrs, including St. Teresa of Ávila, Spain, reformer of Carmelite Order, writer, mystic. Remembered October 15.
Tere, Teresita (Theresa)

Tita Lat. (fem. **Tito**)

Tosca Lat. "Originally of Tuscany, Italy." Spanish for "strong." Protagonist of the Puccini opera of the same name.

Tranquilina Lat. (fem. **Tranquilino**) "Tranquil."
Tranquila

Trinidad Lat. "Trinity." The Spanish word for the Holy Trinity.
  Trini
Tristana Cel. (fem. **Tristán**) The protagonist of the novel of the same name by Benito Pérez Galdós, made into a movie directed by Luis Buñuel.
Tulia Lat. (fem. **Tulio**) "Destined for glory."

U

Úrsula Lat. "The Bear." Matriarch of Gabriel García Márquez's *One Hundred Years of Solitude*, Ursula Iguarán.
Ursulina (Ursula)

Una Lat. "The only one." From Spanish *única* or "unique." A saint and descendent of the duke of Alsace who was recognized for washing the clothing of the poor and dubbed "Santa Lavandera" (washer).

V

Valentina Lat. (fem. **Valentín**) "Strong."
Tina, Val, Valencia, Valera, Valina

Valeria Lat. (fem. **Valerio**) "Healthy and robust." A saint who suffered martyrdom during early Christianity, remembered in Milan on April 26.
Valeriana

Vanessa Character in Jonathan Swift's *Gulliver's Travels*.
Vanesa

Vanina Heb. A nickname for Giurannina or **Juanita**.

Venerada Lat. (fem. **Venerado**) "Venerated."
Veneradina, Veneradita

Ventura Lat. A nickname of **Buenaventura**, which means "will be happy."

Venus Lat. Roman goddess of beauty and love.
Venus, Venusita

Vera Lat. "Truth." A character from *A Hero for Our Time* by Mikhail Lermontov (1814–41).
Verana, Verbena, Verena

Verónica Var. **Vernice**. In the Bible, the name of the young girl who wiped Jesus' face on his way to Calvary. The cloth she used later showed a clear image of his face. Mexican actress Verónica Castro.

Vicenta It. (fem. **Vicente**) "One who overcomes."
Victoria Lat. (fem. **Victor**) "Victory." A queen of England.
Vicki, Vicky, Victoriana, Victorina
Vilma OE. A nickname of **Guillermina**.
Violeta Lat. The flower whose name was used for the protagonist of the opera by Francisco Mara Piave with the music of Guiseppe Verdi entitled *La Traviata*. Nicaraguan President Violeta Chamorro.
Virginia Lat. "She has the attributes of a virgin." A character in the novel *Paul and Virginia* by J. H. Bernardin de Saint-Pierre. Writer Virginia Woolf.
Visitación Lat. "Visitation." An order of nuns. Technically the word recalls the visit St. Mary paid to her cousin St. Isabel, remembered by the church on July 2.
Víveca Scan. "Alive."
Vivian Cel. (fem. **Viviano**) "Full of life."
Viv, Vivian, Vivianna, Vivien (Vivian)

Wanda Slavic. "Wanderer."

Xaviera Basque. (fem. **Xavier**) "New home."
 Xavyera, Zaviera
Xenia Gr. "The hospitable foreign guest."
 Zena, Zenia, Zina
Xilma Ger. Var. **Selma.** "Helmet."
Ximena Sp. Var. of **Jimena.** "Heard."

Yamila Arab "Beautiful."

Yemina Lat. A Spanish variation of **Gémina**.

Yoconda It. "Happy, jovial." Spanish version of Giaconda. Leonardo da Vinci's *La Giaconda*.

Yolanda Gr. "Violet flower." The Spanish version of Violet.
   Ilantha, Iola, Iolanda, Jolan, Jolana, Jolanta, Yola

Ysabel Heb. Var. Isabel. "Pledged to God."
   (Elizabeth)

Yvette Ger. Dim. Yvonne. "Yew wood."
   Ivette

Yvonne Ger. "Yew wood."

Z

Zarela Popular var. **Sara**.
Zahira Arab. "Shining, brilliant."
   Zahirita
Zandra Var. **Sandra**. Dim. **Alexandra**.
Zarola Arab. "The hunter." Daughter of the Moorish king of Seville, Benavet, who changed her name to Isabel when she became a Christian.
Zelma Ger. Dim. **Anselma**. "Helmet."
Zenaida Gr. "Consecrated by God." Patron saint of Constantinople, remembered October 11.
Zenobia Prob. from Gr. (fem. **Zenobio**) Wife of the great Spanish poet and Nobel laureate Juan Ramón Jiménez.
Zita Per. Sita, heroine of *Ramayana*, the great epic poem of ancient India. An Italian saint who is the patron of domestics, remembered April 27.
Zoe Gr. "Full of life." Two empresses of the East, one the wife of Leon VI, the other of Roman II.
Zoila Gr. (fem. **Zoilo**) "Has life."
Zoraida Arab. "The eloquent." A character from a tragedy by N. Álvarez Centeno set during the time the Moors dominated Spain.
Zuleika Arab. "Lovely."
Zulma Arab. "Healthy and vigorous."
   Zulema

II

Names for Boys

Nombres de Niños

A

Aarón Heb. "The inspirator." In the Old Testament, Moses' older brother, who went with the Israelites into the desert and was one of their high priests.
Aaran, Aaren, Ari, Arín, Aron, Ron, Ronnie, Ronny

Ábaco Per. A martyred saint of the Catholic church whose feast is celebrated January 19.
Aba, Abaquito, Baco

Abán Per. Benevolent genie in Persian mythology who had powers over water and the arts.
Aba, Abanito

Abás Myth. A centaur, who fought against the Lipitites.
Aba

Abdallah Arab. "Servant of God."
Ab, Abdel, Abdul

Abdías Heb. "Servant of God." Obadiah, minor biblical prophet, author of the book of the Old Testament that bears his name.

Abdón Heb. Arab. "Very obsequious." In the Bible, he was sent by God to stop the people from worshiping false idols. A judge of Israel. A martyr whose feast is celebrated July 30.
Don, Donny

Abel Heb. "Breath." The second son of Adam and

Eve, who was murdered in the Bible by his brother Cain.

Abé, Able

Abelardo Celt. Became popular because of the twelfth-century French philosopher and theologist Pierre Abélard, who fell in love with and seduced his student, Héloïse. Her uncle and guardian had him emasculated, even though he married Héloïse. She became a nun and he became a monk. Puerto Rican folk writer Abelardo Díaz Alfaro.

Ab, Abbey, Abby, Abel (Abelard)

Abercio Gr. Lat. Catholic saint and Bishop of Hierapolis. His feast is celebrated October 22.

Abías Heb. "My father is God." Several biblical figures, including the son of a King of Judea who died in 955 B.C.

Abiah, Abija, Abijah

Abilio Lat. "Harbors no animosity." Catholic saint, second bishop of Alexandria, successor of Marcus. His feast is celebrated February 22.

Abimael Heb. "Father is God." Peruvian Abimael Guzmán, head of Latin American guerrilla group Sendero Luminoso (The Shining Path).

(Abimel)

Abo Heb. "Father." Abbo of Fleury, Catholic saint whose feast is celebrated November 13.

Abraham Heb. "Father of nations." First of the Hebrew partriarchs. In the Bible, Abraham and his wife Sarah have a son, Isaac, when they are 100 and 90 years old, respectively. U.S. President Abraham Lincoln.

Abrahamo, Abrahán, Abram, Abrami, Abramo, Abran, Avron, Ibrahim

Abril Lat. Second month of the ancient Roman calendar. (The year began with March.) Name of two martyrs. Rarely used as a boy's name these days.

Absalón Heb. "Father of Peace." In the Bible, the third son of King David. His story is told in the second book of Samuel.
Absalán, Absolón (Absolom)

Acacio Gr. "Without malice." Saint from the third century who was the bishop of Antioch and who the Catholic Church of Asia remembers on March 31.

Acis Myth. Son of Faunus and the nymph Symacthis, who fell in love with the nymph Galatea.

Acteón Myth. Son of Aristeus and Autonoe, educated by the centaur Chiron.
(Acton)

Adad Myth. "One or unique." The Mesopotamian god of storms.
Aeda

Adalberto Ger. "Of the nobility." Adalbert, three saints of the Catholic Church, remembered on April 23, June 20, and June 25.
Adal, Adalard, Adalbe, Bert, Berto

Adalgiso Ger. "The lance of nobility." St. Adalgiso, priest and hermitage of the seventh century. Adelchi was King of the Lombards and a staunch enemy of Charlemagne who died in 788. Adelchi is the title of a tragedy by Alessandro Manzoni.

Adán Heb. "Son of red earth." In the Bible, the first man God created. God made him out of earth and then breathed life into him.
Adamo, Adao, Adam, Addie, Addis, Addison, Addy, Adnon

Adelardo Ger. "Noble and courageous."
Adal, Adel, Adelard, Adelino

Adelio Ger. "The father of the noble prince."
Adelo

Adelmar Ger. "He is famous because of his noble lineage."

Adelmo Ger. "Noble protector." Aidhelm, Catholic saint, bishop of Sherborne. His feast is celebrated May 25.

Adhemar Ger. "He is illustrious for his fights." French prelate of the eleventh century. Promoter and spiritual director of the first Crusade.

Adiel Heb. "Adorned by God." Biblical figure, descended from the tribe of Simeon.

Admeto Gr. Admetus was informed by Pelias that he would attain immortality if he found someone that would offer to die in his place. His wife, Alcestes, offered herself. The gods accepted the trade and Alcestes went to hell.

Ado Heb. (masc. **Ada**) "Happy." Pious martyr of Rome, bishop of Vienna, France. He is remembered in the French liturgy on December 16.

Adolfo Ger. "Noble wolf." Evolved from Ataulfo, bishop of Westfalia, not formally canonized, but considered a saint there. His feast is celebrated on February 14. Also, Spanish poet Gustavo Adolfo Bécquer and Adolf Hitler.
Adolf, Adolfus, Adolph, Adophe, Adolpho, Adolphus, Dolfo, Dolphus (Adolph)

Adonai Heb. "My lord." The Hebrew designation for divinity.

Adonias Heb. "My father is Jehovah." Adonijah, biblical figure, brother of Solomon, who had him executed for committing a crime.

Adonis Gr. "The most beautiful man." In Greek mythology, a young man of extraordinary beauty raised by the nymphs with whom Aphrodite fell in love.

Adrián Lat. "Native of Adria," an Italian city. Various Catholic saints, including Pope Adrian, the only English pope (1154–59), remembered July 8.
Ade, Adiano, Adrien, Hadrian, Hadrien, Hadrieno

Adriel Heb. Member of the Assembly of God.

Agamemnón Gr. "Works slowly." Chief of the Trojan Greeks, man of firm will. He was the most powerful prince of Greece and directed the Greek army during the Trojan War.
Agamenón

Agapito Heb. "The beloved." Various saints and martyrs, including Pope Agapetus I, called the "trumpet of evangelism and herald of justice." Remembered April 22.
Agaopio

Agatón Gr. "The good one." Mythological figure. Catholic saint, pope, born in Sicily of Greek parents, who distinguished himself by his generosity and gentleness. Remembered January 10.

Agenor Gr. "Strong and virile." Mythological figure, son of Poseidon and Libya. A character in *The Iliad*.

Ageo Heb. "Funny, strong." Haggai, one of the minor prophets of the Old Testament.

Agesilao Gr. "The conductor of the people." Surname of Hades, name of two kings of Sparta.

Agevarén Tib. "God of the harvest."

Agnián Brazil. "A mean spirit."
Aquián

Agoyo Guinea. "God of good advice."

Agua Sp. "Water." Adored as a god by almost all ancient people. The beginning of all things, according to some Greek philosophers.

Agni Hindi. "God of fire."

Agrícola Lat. "He who cultivates the land." Spanish for "agricultural." Three Catholic saints, one who is a martyr remembered on November 4.

Agrico

Agripino Gr. "Born with his feet out front." Catholic saint, bishop of Naples who is remembered for his many miracles. His feast is celebrated November 9.

Agripo, Agripito

Agustín Lat. "He deserves veneration." St. Augustine, one of the church's greatest philosophers and theologians, whose feast is celebrated August 28.

Austen, Austin (Augustine or Augustus)

Aidano Gaelic. For some, the masc. of **Aída.** Aidan, Irish saint, bishop of the island of Lindisfarne, now Saint Island.

(Aidan)

Aimón Ger. "Homebody." A saint and devoted Dominican remembered by the church April 30 and August 5. Literary figure immortalized by Ariosto.

(Aimon or Eamon)

Alá Arab. Muslim name for God.

Aladino Ger. Aladdin, sultan and protagonist of the *Arabian Nights*, whose magic lamp made wishes come true.

(Alladin)

Alán Ger. The Alans, who invaded Spain in the fifth century.

Al, Alan, Alanito, Alano, Allan, Allen

Alarico Ger. "King of all." Alaric, two famous Visigoth kings, the first who pillaged Rome but respected the temples.

Albán Ger. St. Alban, the first Christian martyr of Great Britain, remembered on June 20. From Alba, an ancient Latin city.
Al, Albano, Albin, Albion, Alvan, Alvin (Alban)

Alberico Ger. "Prince of the elves." In Nordic mythology, elf that guarded the treasures of the Nibelungs. St. Alberic, eleventh century abbot and one of the founders of the Order of Cister.

Alberto Ger. "Eternally brilliant." St. Albert the Great, Dominican friar and bishop, teacher of St. Thomas, whose feast is celebrated November 15. Writer Albert Camus. Prince Albert, consort of Queen Victoria of England. Argentine singer Alberto Cortéz.
Adalberto, Aliberto, Berto (Albert)

Albino Lat. "Fair-skinned and fair-haired." Spanish for "albino." Catholic saint and martyr, remembered June 21.
(Albin)

Alceo Gr. "The strong man." In Greek mythology, the grandfather of Hercules and two sons of Hercules.

Alcibíades Gr. "Strong and brave." Celebrated Athenian general and politician who lived in the fifth century B.C. Disciple of Socrates. Saint and martyr of the Galias, remembered June 7.

Alcides Gr. "Strong, vigorous and energetic." Surname given to Hercules and his descendants because they were the grandchildren of Alceo, mythological son of Perseus.

Alcuino Ger.-Lat. "Friend of the temple." English saint (735–804) who wrote several treatises on grammar and was one of the most eminent scholars of the eighth century, remembered by the

Catholic Church on May 19. Teacher of Charlemagne.

Aldemar Ger. "Experienced." Italian saint celebrated by the Catholic Church on March 24.

Alderico Ger. "Noble prince." Catholic saint whose feast is celebrated January 7.

Aldo Ger. (masc. **Alda**) "Beautiful."

Alejandrino Gr. (masc. **Alejandrina**) "Protector." Der. **Alejandro**.

Alejandro Gr. "He who shelters others." Famous Greek general "Alexander the Great," king of Macedonia and founder of a vast empire. Son of Philip II, who conquered Greece, Phoenicia, Egypt, and Persia. Various saints and martyrs of the Catholic Church. Bishop of Alexandria, remembered February 26.

Al, Alaster, Alejandro, Alejo, Alek, Ales, Alesandre, Alesandro, Alesandros, Alesi, Alesio, Alesis, Alessandro, Alex, Alexis, Alic, Alik, Alistar, Alister, Sacha, Sander, Sandro (Alexander)

Alejo Gr. "The protector." Two saints of the Catholic church whose feasts are celebrated February 12 and July 17. Cuban writer Alejo Carpentier.

Alepio Gr. "One who doesn't lack flavor." A saint, friend of St. Augustine, remembered on August 15.

Alipio

Alexis Lat. Var. **Alepio**. The central character of the novel *Zorba the Greek* by Nikos Kazantzakis. Also a bishop of Kiev in the fourteenth century.

Alfeo Gr. In mythology, Alpheus is a river god who pursues Arethusa until she is changed into a stream by Artemis. In the Bible, the father of apostle St. James.

(Alfie)

Alfio Gr. "The one with the white skin." Poet during the times of Tiberius, character from *Cavallería Rusticana* by Giovanni Verga. Catholic saint and martyr, remembered on May 10.
(Alfie)

Alfonso Ger. "Always prepared to fight." Several Catholic saints, including St. Alphonsus Liguori, remembered August 1.
Alfie, Alfo, Alfonzo, Alonso, Alonzo, Alphonso, Fonso, Fonzi (Alphonse)

Alfredo Ger. "Peace." Alfred the Great, Anglo-Saxon king.

Alí Arab. "Sublime." Nephew of Muhammad the prophet. Name used by many of Spain's Arab conquerors.

Alonso Var. Alfonso. A protagonist in the famed Spanish novel *Don Quijote* by Miguel de Cervantes Saavedra. A Spanish saint who spent most of his life in Mallorca and is remembered there on October 30.
(Alonzo)

Alterio Gr. "The one who has a good future."

Alucio Lat. "Brilliant or lucid." An Italian saint remembered on October 23.

Alvar Var. Álvaro

Álvaro Ger. "Completely cautious." Spanish saint known as St. Álvaro of Córdoba, remembered on February 19. Protagonist of the romantic drama *Don Álvaro o la Fuerza del Sino* by the Duque de Rivas (1791–1865).

Alveo Chilean-Indian. "God of death."

Alvino Ger. "Friend of the elves."
Alvin

Amadeo Lat. "He who loves God." Three Catholic saints bear this name. Their feast days are January 28, February 12, and March 30. Portuguese devout who founded the congregation of Amedeistas in Milan. Wolfgang Amadeus Mozart. **(Amadeus)**

Amadís Lat. "The great love." Paradigm of love. Amadis of Gaul, hero of a sixteenth-century Spanish romance of chivalry.

Amado Lat. "He who is the object of love." In Spanish the past tense of *amar*, "to love." St. Amado of Sión, remembered December 13.

Amador Lat. "He who professes love." St. Amador, hermit, and St. Amador, bishop of Auxerre, Catholic saints remembered on August 20 and May 1, respectively.

Amalio Modern. (masc. **Amalia**)

Amancio It. "Lover of God." Martyred saint, remembered June 10.

Amandio Il. Var. **Amancio**.

Amando Lat. "He who is loving." St. Amando, bishop of Bordeaux, and St. Amand, Apostle of Flanders, who are remembered on June 18 and February 6, respectively.

Amaranto Gr. "He who doesn't flounder." Christian martyr, unofficially remembered on October 28.

Amaru Quechua. "Snake, boa." Túpac Amaru Inca warrior who was executed by the Spaniards.

Ambrosio Gr. "The immortal." St. Ambrose, bishop of Milan, fourth century. A great pastor whose feast is celebrated December 7.

Amelio Var. **Amalio**.

Américo Ger. "The acting prince." Celebrated Italian navigator Amerigo Vespucci (1454–1512) who gave his name to the new continent discovered by Christopher Columbus.

Amida Myth. Japan. King of the skies and eternal happiness.

Amílcar Gr. Hamilcar Barea, Carthaginian general, father of Hannibal, who began the conquest of Spain in the third century B.C.

Amín Arab. "The faithful man."

Amintor Gr. "The protector."

Amón Heb. "The mysterious." Ammon, name of various biblical characters, among them the son of Lot, brother of Moab, considered the father of the Ammonites. Derived from Greek, the main god of the Egyptians, identified with Zeus in Greek mythology and Jupiter in Roman mythology.

Monito, Mono (Aimon)

Amos Heb. "Robust." Third of the minor biblical prophets, brother of King Amasías and father of Isaiah, who was the first to state his message in writing.

Anacleto Gr. "He who is called upon." First century pope.

Ananías Heb. "Given by the grace of God." Saint cited by St. Paul during the miracle of his conversion. The Greeks remembered him on October 1, and the Latins on October 25, the day of St. Paul's conversion.

Anan, Anani

Anastasio Gr. "The resurrected." A dozen martyrs and saints bear this name, including Pope Anastasio I, whose feast is celebrated December 19. Nicaraguan general Anastasio Somoza.

Anastas, Anasto, Anastos, Stasio (Anastasius)

Anatolio Gr. "From the Orient." Three saints bear this name, including the patriarch of Constantinople who is remembered on July 3.

Anatol, Anatolo (Anatole)

Andrés Gr. "Manly." Prince Andrey, character from Leo Tolstoy's *War and Peace*. Various Catholic saints and martyrs also bear this name, including Andrew the Apostle, brother of St. Peter who evangelized the south of Russia, whose feast is celebrated November 30. Spanish guitarist Andrés Segovia.
Andras, Andre, Andris (Andy or Andrew)

Androcles Gr. "Glorious man." Roman slave of a well-known legend who was condemned to be put to death and was thrown to the lions. A grateful lion whose paw he had cleaned of thorns freed him.

Andrónico Gr. "Victorious man." A Greek architect who invented the weather vane. Two Catholic saints by this name are remembered October 9 and 22. Name of various emperors of Constantinople.

Andros Pol. "God of the sea."

Ángel Gr. "The messenger." Guardian angels are remembered on October 2.

Angelino Lat. (masc. **Angelina**) "Like an angel."

Angilberto Comb. form **Angel** and **Alberto**.

Aniano Gr. (masc. **Ania**) A saint, bishop of Alexandria, remembered April 26.

Aníbal Punic. "God is favorable." Hannibal, famous Carthaginian commander who invaded Thalia and Spain but was defeated by Scipio Africanus.

Aniceto Gr. "The invincible." Anicetus, saint and martyr, Catholic pope who ascended to the chair of St. Peter during the reign of Emperor Anthony Pious, second century. His feast is celebrated April 17.

Anisio Gr. (var. **Aniceto**) "One who keeps his

word." Saint, bishop of Thessalonia, named Patriarch Vicar of Iliria by Pope, Saint Dámaso. His feast day is celebrated December 30.

Anón Gr. "Graceful." Bishop of Colonia who is remembered by the church December 4.

Ansaldo Ger. "God reigns in me." Two saints remembered on February 2 and August 5.

Anselmo Ger. "God is my helmet." Various Catholic saints, including St. Anselm, archbishop of Canterbury, doctor of the church, and one of the greatest wise men of the epoch, twelfth century. His feast is April 21.
Ansel, Elmo

Antenor Gr. "He who fights back." A mythological hero of Troy, described in the *Iliad* as a prudent advisor and advocate of peace. Trojan prince. Mythical founder of Padua.

Anteo Gr. "Son of the Earth and Neptune." Antaeus had a marvelous strength that was renewed every time he touched the Earth, his mother.

Antero Gr. "Flowery." Saint, pope, and martyr who was the first to order, to write up, and preserve the acts of the martyrs. Remembered January 3.

Antioco Gr. "The one who opposes."

Antonio Lat.-Gr. "The flourishing." Various saints, martyrs of the church, including St. Anthony of Padua (1195–1231), doctor of the church, celebrated June 13. Portuguese Franciscan who preached in France, Italy, and Africa. Member of Roman triumvirate, Marc Anthony, ally of Caesar and lover of Cleopatra who was immortalized by Shakespeare. St. Anthony Abad (251–356), Egyptian hermit who suffered many temp-

tations in the desert and founded a monastery. Spanish Fascist Antonio Primo de Rivera. Spanish actor Antonio Banderas. Latin American liberator Antonio José de Sucre, Cuban liberator Antonio Maceo. Spanish artist Antonio Tapies.
Antolín, Antolino, Antonito, Antony, Ton, Toni, Tonito, Tony (Anthony)

Antulio Comb. form **Antonio** and **Tulio.**

Apeles Gr. "Occupant of sacred ground." One of the most celebrated painters of ancient times.

Apolinar Lat. From Apollo, St. Apolinar, Bishop of Hierapolis and famous Christian professor of the second century, remembered January 8.
Apolinario, Apollos, Apolon, Apolos

Apolo Lat. God of music, poetry, arts, medicine and prophecy represented as exemplifying manly youth and beauty.
(Apollo)

Apolodoro Gr. "Gift from Apollo." Name of Greek artists and wisemen, among them the fifth century sculptor and the second century historian. A disciple of Socrates cited in *The Apology*.

Apolonio Lat. "Follower of Apollo." Apollonius, a biblical character, a general defeated by Judas Macabee. A martyred saint remembered April 18.

Apuleyo Lat. Lucius Apuleius, philosopher and poet from the second century A.D., author of *The Golden Ass*.

Aquiles Gr. "Without lips." Achilles, mythological hero of Homer's *Iliad*. Leader of the Thessalonians in the battle of Troy.

Aquilino Lat. "He who has the sharpness of the eagle." Saint, bishop of Evreux, who fought the Visogoths in France and finished his days as a hermit. Remembered October 19.

Arcadio Gr. (masc. **Arcadia**) Two Catholic saints and martyrs remembered January 12 and November 13. Patriarch José Arcadio Buendía in Gabriel García Márquez's novel *One Hundred Years of Solitude*, who married Úrsula and began the Buendía family on which the novel is based.

Arcángel Gr. "Prince of the angels." Title was bestowed on St. Michael, St. Raphael, and St. Gabriel.

Arcelio Lat. (masc. **Aricelia**)

Argentino Lat. "Brilliant and shiny like silver" or "from Argentina."

Argimiro Ger. "Illustrious fighter." Spanish martyr saint during the Muslim domination, celebrated July 28.

Argos Gr. Referred to as Panoptes, which means "he who sees everything," he had one hundred eyes and closed only fifty to sleep.
(Argus)

Ariel Heb. "Little lion of God." A bad angel. A rebelious angel in Milton's *Paradise Lost* and in Goethe's *Faust*. A name for Jerusalem in the Bible. Character from William Shakespeare's *The Tempest*.
Arel, Arielo

Arión Gr. "Very esteemed." Famous musician from Greek mythology who is mentioned repeatedly by Ovid.

Aristides Gr. "The best of all men." Various figures of Greek antiquity, including St. Aristides, an Athenian philosopher who converted to Christianity.

Aristóbulo Gr. "The best counselor." Five kings of

Judea. Distinguished general Alexander the Great. A disciple of the apostle mentioned in the New Testament.

Arístocles Gr. "Possesses great glory." A saint remembered June 23. Original name of Philosopher Plato.

Aristófanes Gr. Aristophanes, renowned Greek writer of satirical comic dramas. Aristophanes of Byzantium, famous grammarian who standardized the accents in the Greek language.

Armando Ger. "The warrior." Armand, the Alexandre character in Dumas novel *Camille*. Actor Armand Assante.
Arman, Armande, Armin, Armon, Armond, Armonde, Armondo (Armand)

Arnaldo Ger. "That has the power of the eagle."
Arne, Arni, Waldo (Arnaud or Arnold)

Arnoldo Comb. form **Arnaldo** with **Arnolfo**.
(Arnold)

Arnolfo Ger. "Wolf and eagle." St. Arnulf, bishop of Metz admired for his prudence and his bravery in battle, celebrated on July 18.
Arnulfo

Arquibaldo Ger. "Brave and audacious." Saint, bishop of London remembered by Catholics on April 30.

Arquímides Gr. "Profound thinker." Archimedes, scientist and mathematician, born in the ancient Greek city of Syracuse.

Arsenio Gr. "Vigorous, virile." St. Arsenio the Great, remembered in the Armenian rite on July 19. Thief Arsenio Lupin, main character in a long series of novels by Belgian writer Maurice Leblanc (1864–1914). Talk show host Arsenio Hall.

Artaldo Ger. "The protector." Bishop of Belley, remembered on October 7th.

Artemio Gr. "Honest, intact." Two martyred saints remembered on January 25 and October 20.
(Artemis)

Arturo Celt. "Noble bear." Arthur, one of the legendary knights of the Round Table, and various princes of Britain. Arturo, protagonist and narrator of the novel by Colombian José Eustacio Rivera, *The Vortex*.
Art, Arti, Artie, Arturito, Turito, Turío, Turo (Arthur)

Atahualpa Peru. Son of Huayna Capac, the last emperor of the Incas. He was killed by the Spaniards in 1533 in a battle that marks the beginning of the end of the Inca Empire. Atahualpa Yupanqui, Argentine singer-songwriter.

Atalo Gr. "Youthful." Two saints remembered on March 10 and June 2.

Atanasio Gr. "Immortal." Various saints, among them Athanasius, bishop of Alexandria, celebrated on May 2nd.

Ático Gr. "Inhabitant of Attica (Athens)." Roman knight, Tito Pomponio Atico, friend of Cicero. Saint, patriarch of Constantinople, who died in the fifth century and is remembered on January 8th.

Atila Gothic. "The little father."

Atilano Ger. Der. **Atila**. Saint, bishop of Zamora, Spain, who lived during the first years of the Spanish reconquest from the Moors. Remembered on October 3.

Atilio Lat. "With crooked feet." One of the great characters of the legendary history of Rome, *Atilio Régulo*, who also created and inspired poetry.

Auberto Ger. "Of brilliant nobility." Two saints re-

membered on September 10 and December 10.
(Aubrey)

Audelino Ger. "Famous prince."

Augusto Lat. "Worthy of respect." Augustus, Roman emperor at the time Jesus Christ was born. Two devout martyrs of the church celebrated on February 17 and November 6, respectively. Nicaraguan rebel Augusto Sandino.
Agostino, Agosto, Agustín, Agustino, Augie,
Augustas, Auguste, Augustino, Augusto

Aureliano Lat. From the Aurelius family. Saint, bishop of Arles, remembered on June 16. Roman Emperor from the third century. Colonel Aureliano Buendía, second son of José Arcadio Buendía and Ursula in Garbriel García Márquez's *One Hundred Years of Solitude*. Aureliano has seventeen sons, all named Aureliano.

Aurelio Lat. "Golden." Roman Emperor Marcus Aurelius, who died in A.D 180. Two saints of the Catholic Church, St. Aurelio of Carthage and St. Aurelio, martyred with Natalia, remembered on June 16 and July 27, respectively. Baseball player Aurelio Rodríguez.
(Aurelius)

Avelino Lat. "From Arella (Italy)." St. Andrew Avellino, remembered on November 10.

Avito Lat. "Pertaining to the grandfather." Two saints remembered on June 17 and February 15th.

Azarías Heb. "God holds me."
Arariah

B

Bábilas Lat. "Door of God." Babylas, Catholic saint, martyr, bishop of Antioch, remembered on January 24.
Babil, Babito, Balbo

Balbino Lat. "Stammering, stuttering." Catholic saint remembered on March 3. From *balbus*, which refers to babbling and other speech impediments.

Baldomero Ger. "Famous, fighter." French blacksmith who became a monk in Lyon, considered the patron of blacksmiths, remembered on February 27.
Baldemar

Balduino Ger. "Brave friend."

Baltasar Gr. "Protected by God." Balthazar, one of the three kings who followed a guiding star to the place where Jesus was born in Jerusalem. Celebrated by the Church on January 6. The three kings tradition used to be much stronger than Santa Claus in the Spanish-speaking world. Two saints, Baltasar of Chiavari and Baltasar of Torres, remembered on October 25 and June 1.
Balto, Bathasar

Bardo Ger. "Poet." St. Bardo of Mainz, a west

German city on the Rhine, remembered on June 5.

Bardón

Barlaam Heb. "Town elder." Legendary saint, who along with St. Josafat, is one of the main characters of the Christian version of the Siddhartha Buddha legend. Saint martyr of Antioch, celebrated on November 19.

Barbero, Barleem, Barlow

Baroncio Lat. "Baron." Saint famous for his visions of the supernatural, remembered on March 25.

Bartolomé Heb. "Farmer's son." St. Bartholomew, martyr, one of the twelve apostles. Remembered on August 24. The Spanish missionary Bartolomé de las Casas wrote about the excesses of the Spanish Conquest in Latin America.

Bartel, Bartho, Bartolomeo (Bartholomew)

Baruc Heb. "Blessed by God." Baruch, scribe who is supposed to have authored the biblical book of the same name.

Baruch

Basiano Gr. "Sharp judgment." Saint, bishop of Lodi, who fought tenaciously against the Arians. Remembered on January 19.

Basilio Gr. "Sovereign, King." Greek emperor Basil II (965–1025) who reigned during a very powerful time for the Byzantine Empire. Various saints, among which is Basil the Great, one of the four Fathers of the Greek church, celebrated on January 2.

Basile, Basilus, Bazil (Basil)

Baudilio Ger. "Audacious, brave." Martyr saint whose tomb was once one of the most famous sanctuaries of Provence, decapitated for refuting the pagans. Celebrated in France on May 20.

Bautista Gr. "Baptizer." St. John the Baptist, the last Hebrew prophet, who baptized Jesus in the Jordan River. Celebrated June 24. In Spanish, San Juan Bautista, after whom the capital of Puerto Rico, San Juan, was named.
Tito

Beda Ger. "The one who disposes and orders." English saint, Bede the Venerable, monk, scholar, historian, named Doctor of the Church in 1899. Remembered on May 27.

Belarmino It. "The one with the beautiful armor." St. Robert Bellarmine, Italian cardinal and theologist, canonized by Pope Pious eleventh, remembered on May 13.

Belindo It. (masc. **Belinda**) "Attractive." Saint, bishop of Padua, patron of Adria, Italy, remembered on November 26.

Belisario Gr. "The swordsman." Belisarius, a general of Emperor Justinian who after being accused of conspiracy went from glory in the army to misery in jail. Also from the Greek word for "arrow." Colombian politician Belisario Betancourt.

Beltrán Ger. "The one with the dashing shield." Two saints, remembered on September 6 and October 16. Also a Shakespearean character.
Bertran, Betran

Ben Arab. "Son." Der. **Benjamín**.

Benedicto Lat. "The blessed one." A dozen popes, including a saint, Benedict II, celebrated on May 8. Character in Shakespeare's *Much Ado About Nothing*. Spanish writer Benito Pérez Galdós.
Ben, Benito (Benedict)

Benigno Lat. "Benevolent, kind-hearted." Two saints remembered on November 1 and 7.

Benjamín Heb. "The son of the last days." In Genesis, the last of the twelve children of Jacob and Rachel. Popular name for the last son of a family. Cuban musician Benny Moré.
Ben, Beniamino, Benjaman, Benjamen, Benjamino, Benji, Benjiman, Benny, Benyamin, Benyamino (Benjamin)

Bernabé Aramaic. "Son of the prophecy." St. Barnabas of Cyprus, companion of St. Paul who was considered an apostle by the first fathers, even though Jesus did not select him, because the Holy Spirit had entrusted him with a special mission. Remembered on June 11.
Barbabas, Barnabé, Barnabee, Barney, Barní

Bernardo Ger. "Rash, like a bear." Bernardo del Carpio, heroic Spanish mythical character, whose adventures have been celebrated by various renowned Spanish writers. Name of two famous medieval saints. One a founder of a monastic order; the other, for whom the shaggy brown-and white-dogs are named, is patron saint of mountain climbers.
Barney, Bernardito, Bernardo (Bernard)

Bernardino Various saints of the Catholic Church, among them Bernardino of Siena, famous for his extraordinary apostolic labor. Remembered on May 20.

Berno Ger. "Rash." Saint, abbot of Cluny, remembered on January 13.

Berto OE. (masc. **Berta**) Short for **Alberto** and **Lamberto**.
Bertoldo (Burt)

Besarión Gr. "The walker." Egyptian saint greatly venerated in the Orient who performed miracles and spent his life going from one place to the other. In Orient celebrated on June 6, but the Roman martyrology remembers him on June 17.

Bienvenido Lat. "Admitted with gaiety." The Spanish word for "welcome."

Bladimiro Ger. "Famous for his power." From the Russian Vladimir.

Blas Lat. "Stammers." St. Blaise, bishop martyr of Sebaste, Albania, born in 316 A.D., remembered on February 3.

Bonifacio Lat. "Does the right thing." Nine popes, including two saints, Bonifacio I and Bonifacio IV. Various saints, including Winfrith, apostle of Germany, remembered on June 5. Cuban poet Bonifacio Byrne.
(Bonificent)

Boris Slav. "Warrior." Bloodthirsty sixteenth-century Czar Boris Godunov on which Russian composer Mussorgsky based an opera and Russian playwright Pushkin based a drama. Also, Boris Becker, Boris Yeltsin.

Braulio Ger. "Glitters, glows." Saint, bishop of Zaragoza, Spain, remembered on March 26. Puerto Rican actor Braulio Castillo.

Brendano Ger. "The one who carries the torch." Brendan, Irish saint who founded a monastery and received his instructions from an angel. Remembered with big festivities on May 16 in Ireland.
(Brendan)

Brian Celtic. "The strong one." One of the martyrs of London in 1591, remembered on December 10. Character in the epic poem *The Captive* by Esteban Echeverría.

Bricio Lat. "Strong." St. Brice, a disciple of St. Martin.

Bruno Lat. "Brown skin." Various saints, among them the noted founder of the Carthusian Order, remembered on October 6. Bruno Diaz was the Spanish name given Batman.

Bucardo Ger. "Defender of the fortress." St. Burchard, first bishop of Wurzburg, remembered on October 14.

Buenaventura Lat. "Good legacy." Various saints, among them St. Buenaventura known as Dr. Seráfico, a great Italian Franciscan clergyman, writer, and theologian whose feast is celebrated on July 14.
(Bonaventure)

Bulmaro Ger. "The strong combatant." Saint, abbot of monastery of the same name in Picardia, remembered on July 20.

C

Caledonio Lat. "From Caledonia." In northern Scotland, he is a saint remembered on March 3.
Caldito, Donio, Donito, Donny

Calistrato Gr. "The one who leads a great army." Calistratius, famous Athenian speaker from the fourth century B.C. Saint remembered on September 26.

Calixto Gr. "Beautiful." Pope and martyr, St. Calixtus I, celebrated on October 14. Main character in Fernando de Rojas's *Tragicomedy of Calixto and Melibea*.
Calisto, Callisto

Calócero Gr. (var. **Calógero**)

Calógero Gr. "Old, wise." St. Calógero, fourth century Sicilian hermit, remembered on May 19. In modern Greek, it has come to signify "monk."

Camilo Lat. "Novice to priesthood." Various saints, among them, St. Camillus of Lellis, Italian monk who founded the Ministers of the Sick. Remembered on July 14. Spanish writer Camilo José Cela.
Camilito

Cancio Lat. "From the noble Roman family of Ancios." Martyr, with his brother Canciano and sister Cancianila, for refusing to give up their Christian faith, remembered on May 31.

Canciano, Canziano

Cándido Lat. "Pure, white." He is immaculate, brilliant, and white. Saint remembered on September 22.

Carim Arab. "Generous."

Karim

Carlos Ger. "Strong, manly." About ten saints from the Catholic Church, among them St. Charles of Borroneo, archbishop of Milan, protector of the arts, who is remembered on November 4. Very popular Spanish name. Also the name of various kings and emperors: Prince Charles of England, King Juan Carlos of Spain, Carlos I of Spain, and Emperor Charles V. Mexican writer Carlos Fuentes. Spanish film director Carlos Saura. Colombian singer Carlos Vives. Argentine singer Carlos Gardel.

Carlito, Carlo, Carloto (Carl)

Carmelo Heb. "Cultivated terrain." Mt. Carmel, where the prophet Elijah lived and where in the twelfth century the convent that housed the order of Carmelites was built. Nuestra Señora del Monte Carmelo (Our Lady of Mount Carmelo). Saint remembered among the martyrs of Damasco on July 10.

Carmelito, Carmo, Milo

Casandro Gr. "Brother of heroes." Cassander, king of Macedonia who took Greece after the death of Alexander the Great.

(Casander)

Casiano Lat. "Equitable, fair." From the family name Casi or Casios. Various saints, among

them, martyr St. Casiano of Imola, remembered on August 13.
Casio

Casimiro Pol. "Preacher of peace." Saint, son of King Casimir IV, prince of Poland, remembered on March 4.

Casio Lat. "The one who wears a helmet." Saint, bishop of Narni, famous for his abnegation and his generosity toward the poor; also a martyr, remembered on June 29 and October 10, respectively.

Casiodoro Gr. "Gift from a friend." Cassiodorus, Roman historian and statesman from the sixth century.

Casto Lat. (dim. **Cástulo**) "Pure, honest." Saint and martyr remembered on May 22.

Cástor Gr. "Brilliant." In mythology, one of the twin sons of Leda that along with his brother Pollux was turned into the constellation Gemini. Castor oil.
Casto
Castorio

Castorio (Lat. var. **Cástor**.) One of the four martyred saints of the fourth century in whose honor a basilica was built in Mount Celio in Rome. Remembered on November 8.
Castorito

Cástulo (Dim. **Casto**) Saint, martyr remembered on March 26.
Castulito, Tulo

Cataldo Ger. "Powerful in war." Catald, Irish saint and patron of Taranto, Italy. Remembered on May 10.
Cataldito, Taldo

Cayetano Lat. "From Gaeta, Italy." St. Cajetan, founder of the Theatine Order, remembered August 7. Puerto Rican nineteenth-century historian Cayetano Coll y Toste.

Cayo Lat. From the Roman family named Caius, "the happy ones." Three martyred saints, one of them a pope who lived eight years in the Roman catacombs. Remembered on April 22.
Cayito

Cecilio Lat. (masc. **Cecilia**) St. Cecelio, one of the seven men sent to evangelize Spain by St. Peter and St. Paul.
Cecil, Cecilius, Celio

Ceferino Gr. "Gentle like the zephyr." St. Zephyrinus, pope who suffered great persecutions. Remembered on August 26. Argentine Indian, son of the Namuncurá Cacique, venerated as a saint even though he was never beatified.
Ceferito

Celestino Lat. "Inhabitant of the skies." Two sainted popes, Celestine I and Peter Celestine V, remembered on April 6 and May 19, respectively.
Celestito (Celeste)

Celio Lat. Resident of Caelian Hill, one of the seven hills of Rome in the southeast part of the city. Ancient nickname of Jupiter. Roman historian and jurist L. Celio Antipater.

Celso Lat. "High, elevated in the spiritual sense." Various saints, among them, St. Celsus, archbishop of Armagh, celebrated on April 1. Puerto Rican José Celso Barbosa, a famed political supporter of the American annexation of the island.
Celsito

Cenobio St. Cenobio, bishop of Florence, famous for resurrecting five people. Priest and doctor, St. Cenobio, in the city of Sidon, in ancient Phoenicia, remembered on May 25 and February 20, respectively.

César Lat. "Separated from his mother." Julius Caesar, celebrated Roman general and dictator, who conquered the Galias and is considered a military genius of ancient history. Saint, Jesuit priest remembered on April 15. United Farm Worker's founder César Chávez. Cuban composer César Portillo de la Luz. Boxer Julio César Chavez.
(Caesar)

Cesareo Lat. "Follower of Caesar." St. Cesareo, bishop of Arles, remembered on August 27.
Cesario

Cipriano Gr. "From Cypress." St. Cyprian, bishop of Carthage, remembered on September 16. Main character in Calderón de la Barca's (1600–81) *El mágico prodigioso (The Prodigious Magician)*.

Cireneo Gr. "From Cyrene (ancient Greek city in North Africa)." St. Simon of Cyrene, who helped Jesus carry the cross, remembered on December 10.
(Cyrano)

Ciríaco Gr. "Pertaining to God." St. Judas Ciriaco, patron of Ancona, Italy, remembered on May 4.

Cirilo Gr. "Majestic." Der. **Ciro**. St. Cyril, bishop of Alexandria, named Doctor of the Church, remembered on June 27, and St. Cyril, bishop of Jerusalem, remembered on March 18. Cuban writer Cirilo Villaverde.
Ciril

Ciro Gr. "Sir." Saint, martyr, doctor of Alexandria, venerated in Syria, Egypt, and Greece. Remembered on January 31. Ciro II, the great founder of the Persian empire.

Ciselio Lat. "From this side of the sun." Young saint of the fourth century, remembered on August 21.

Claro Gr. "Illustrious, brilliant." St. Claro, first bishop of Nantes, France. St. Claro, abbot of the St. Marcelo monastery in Vienna, remembered on January 1; and St. Claro, priest and martyr, who gave his name to Saint-Clair-Sur-Epte, a French village close to Rouen, remembered on November 4. Spanish word for "clear."
(Clarence)

Claudiano Lat. "Follower of Claudio." Saint and martyr, remembered on February 25.
(Claude)

Claudio Lat. "From the ancient Roman family named Claudios." St. Claudio, bishop of Bensanzón, very popular name in the twelfth century after it was discovered that his body had not deteriorated after five hundred years. Remembered on June 6.
Claudius, Claudio, Klaus (Claud)

Clemente Lat. "Compassionate." St. Clement I, pope and martyr, probably contemporary of Peter and Paul, which is why he is one of the Apostolic Fathers, remembered on November 23. Puerto Rican major-league baseball player Roberto Clemente.
(Clement)

Clementino (masc. **Clementina**) Var. **Clemente**.
(Clementine)

Cleofás Gr. "Vision of glory." One of the disciples before whom the resurrected Jesus appeared on his way to Emaus. One of the twelve disciples.
Cleo, Cleofaso

Cleto Gr. "The chosen." Cletus, saint and martyr.
Cletito

Clodomiro Gr. "Captain of illustrious fame." King of Orleans.
Clod, Clodito, Clodo, Codito, Codo (Claud)

Clodoveo Ger. "Illustrious warrior." Three Frank kings, one of which, Clodoveo I, was converted to Christianity by his wife Clotilde.
Clod, Coldito, Clodo (Claud)

Clovis Ger. Ancient form of Clodoveo.
Clovisito, Clovito (Clovis)

Conrado Ger. "Brave advisor." St. Conrado de Piacenza, advocate of those afflicted with hernias, remembered on February 19. Conrado I, king of Germany in 911. Conrad, hero in English poet Lord Byron's (1788–1824) *The Corsair*.
Conrad, Conradito

Constancio Lat. "Firm, persistent." Constantius, Roman emperor, father of Constantine the Great, who died in 306. Religious man Constancio de Fabiano, remembered on February 25.
Constancito (Constance)

Constantino Lat. Dim. **Constancio**. Roman Emperor Constantine the Great, famous for having converted to Christianity and granting liberty to the church.
Constancito, Constanzo (Constantine)

Cornelio Lat. "From Corne, Italy." Cornelius, centurion converted by St. Peter and who later became bishop of Cesarea. Saint, pope, and martyr, remembered on September 16.
Cornelito (Cornelius)

Cosme Gr. "Clean." Magistrate created in Athens

to balance the power of the king. Cosmas, martyr remembered on September 26.

Cosmito (Cosmo)

Crescencio Lat. "Raised in virtue or sanctity." Various martyrs, the first of whom is remembered on September 14.

Cresci, Crescito (Chris)

Crisanto Gr. "Gold flower."

Cris, Crisito, Santo, Santito (Chris)

Crisóforo Lat. "Having gold or wealth." Two saint martyrs remembered on April 20 and October 25.

Crispín Lat. "With curly hair." St. Crispin, third century Christian martyr, patron saint of shoemakers, remembered on October 25. Henry V fought the battle of Agincourt on his feastday.

Cristián Lat. "Christian, follower of Christ." Christian, two saints, remembered on November 12 and March 18, respectively. Christian Dior.

Cristi, Cristiano, Cristianito, Cristy, Kris, Kristian (Chris or Christian)

Cristóbal Gr. "Carrier of Christ." Saint who used to be represented transporting the baby Jesus in his arms and was considered the patron saint of motorists but today is unofficial. St. Cristóbal of Syria, remembered on July 25. Cristóbal Colón (Christopher Columbus).

Cristi, Cristo (Christopher)

Cruz Lat. "Cross." Catholic celebration of the Holy Cross, remembered on December 14.

Cuauhtémoc "Eagle that descends." Last Aztec emperor.

Custodio Lat. "Guardian angel." The Guardian Angels are celebrated on October 2.

Custi, Custo

D

Dagoberto Ger. "Brilliant like the day." St. Dagoberto II, remembered on December 23. Three Frank kings.
Berto, Dag, Dago, Daguito (Dagwood)

Dalmacio Lat. "From Dalmatia." French religious man who the church remembers on September 26.
Dali, Dalito, Dalmacito, Dalmo

Dalmiro Ger. "Illustrious, noble."
Delmiro, Dolmito

Dámaso Gr. "Skillful animal trainer." Spanish saint and pope in the fourth century, remembered on December 11.
Damito, Damo

Damián Gr. "Glory of the people." St. Peter Damian, promoter of clergy reforms, remembered on February 23.
Dami, Damito (Damien)

Dan Heb. Dim. **Daniel.** "The one who knows how to judge." Former U.S. Vice President Dan Quayle.

Daniel Heb. "God is my judge." Hebrew prophet whose faith saved him in the lion's den and who deciphered the dreams of Nebuchadrezzar. St. Daniel the Stylite, remembered on December 11.

Puerto Rican singer Danny Rivera. Singer Daniel Santos.

Dan, Danal, Danel, Danielito, Danny, Dennis

Danilo Slavic. Var. **Daniel,** incorporated into Spanish.

Danil, Danilito

Dante Lat. Contraction of the ancient Durante. "The constant one." Dante Alighieri, renowned Italian writer from the middle ages, author of *The Divine Comedy*.

Dardo Gr. "Astute, skillful."

Darío Per. "The one who knows how to represent himself." King Darius of Persia who conquered Babylonia, part of India and Europe in the fifth century B.C. Nicaraguan poet Rubén Darío.

David Heb. "The loved one." The second king of Israel and Judah, reputed to be the writer of many psalms, he killed the giant Goliath with his slingshot. Main character in Dickens's (1812–1870) *David Copperfield*.

Daví, Davín, Davis, Davito

Delfín Fr. Dauphin, title given to the firstborn of the king of France. Saint, bishop of Bordeaux, remembered on December 24.

Delfi, Delfito

Delfino Gr. "Dolphin."

Délfor Gr. "From Delfos."

Delfito, Delfo

Demetrio Gr. "Belonging to Demeter, goddess of agriculture and fertility." Various artists, doctors, and thinkers of ancient times. St. Demetrio, martyr of Yugoslavia and St. Demetrio, bishop of Alexandria remembered on October 8 and 9, respectively.

Déme, Meti, Metito (Demetrius)

Deolindo Gr. (masc. **Deolinda**)

Desiderio Lat. "The desired one." Saint Desiderio, bishop of Cahors, remembered in France on November 15. Bandleader and actor Desi Arnaz.
Deri, Derio, Derito, Desi, Desito

Devoto Sp. (masc. **Devota**) "A devoted person."
Devito, Devo

Dídimo Gr. "The twin brother." Didymus, alternate name of the Apostle Thomas, saint and martyr, remembered on April 28.
Didi, Didito, Dino

Diego Sp. (Possibly a derivative of **Santiago**.) Sevillean saint, remembered on November 13 in Spain. Character in French dramatist, Pierre Corneille's (1606–84) *Le Cid*. Mexican painter Diego Rivera. Mexican Indian Juan Diego, to whom Our Lady of Guadalupe, patroness of México, appeared.
Diegito

Dino Heb. (masc. **Dina**) "Shaped in romance." A once popular name, now overtaken by the name given to the Flintstones' pet dinosaur.

Diodoro Gr. "Gift of God." Greek philosopher, Diodoro Cronos. Greek historian Diodoro of Sicily, who authored a history of ancient times. Saint, martyr remembered on December 3.
Dio, Dito, Dorito, Doro

Dionio Lat. (Var. **Dionisio**) Saint remembered on March 16.

Diógenes Gr. "Generated by the God Jove." Greek philosopher, Diogenes the Cynic, famous for searching for a man in the middle of the day with a lantern.
Dio, Genes

Dionisio Gr. "Devoted to Dionysus, god of wine

and revelry." Greek name of the Roman god Bacchus. Saint Dionysius, pope remembered on December 26.

Dioni, Nisio

Dodo Lat. "Aching, suffering." Religious man from the fifteenth century remembered on March 30. Also the extinct bird considered not very bright.

Dudo

Domiciano Lat. (Var. **Domicio**) Saint, bishop of Maastricht who, according to popular belief, killed a terrible monster that was haunting the region, remembered on May 7. Domitian, Roman emperor, the last of the twelve Caesars.

Domi, Domico (Dominic)

Domicio Lat. "Lover of his home."

Domingo Lat. "Devoted to God." Spanish saint Domingo of Guzmán, companion of St. Francis of Assisi and founder of the Order of Friars Preachers, remembered on August 4. The Spanish word for Sunday. Argentinean leader Domingo Faustino Sarmiento.

Domi, Mingo

Donaldo Scot. "World Leader." St. Donald, remembered July 15. The Disney duck and the singer Donny Osmond. Also Donald Trump.

Donal, Donnal, Donnel, Donny, Naldito, Naldo (Donald)

Donato Lat. "Given." St. Donatus, bishop of Fiesole, remembered on October 22.

Donoso (masc. **Donosa**) Saint remembered in Spain on September 2. Spanish publicist and jurisconsult Donoso Cortés. Chilean writer José Donoso.

Donito, Dono, Nosito, Noso

Durante Lat. "Constant, perseverant." Twelfth-century Italian poet, author of *Il Fiore*. The Spanish word for "during." Entertainer Jimmy Durante.
Dante, Danto, Durán, Duranito, Durano, Rante, Rantito

E

Eberardo Ger. "Strong like a bear." A saint and a religious man, remembered on June 22 and August 14, respectively.

Edelberto Ger. "Of illustrious nobility."

Edelmiro Ger. "Celebrated for his nobility."

Edgardo Eng. "The one with the lace who protects property." Edgar, various ancient kings of Scotland and England.
Edgardito (Edgar)

Edmundo Ger. "Defender of property." St. Edmund of Abingdon, archbishop of Canterbury, remembered on November 16.
Eddie, Edmundito (Edmund)

Eduardo Ger. "The one who takes care or waits for land and real estate." Various saints and martyrs, among them St. Edward the Confessor, who never had sexual relations with his wife for his love of God, remembered on October 13. Kings Edward I through VII of England. Name of various princes. Former Colombian president and founder of *El Tiempo* Eduardo Santos. Former president of Chile, Eduardo Frie Montalvo.
(Edward)

Eduino Eng. Saint of great fame because of his miracles and virtues, remembered on October 19.
Edvino

Efigenio Gr. (masc. **Efigenia**) "Of the strong race."

Efraín Heb. "Very fructiferous." Ephraim, second son of Joseph and father of one of the twelve tribes of Israel. Main character in Eugene O'Neill's *Desire Under the Elms*.

Efrén Der. **Efraín**. St. Ephrem of Syria, known for his skills as teacher, poet, preacher, commentator, and defender of the Christian faith, honored as Doctor of the Church, remembered on June 19.
(Efrem)

Egberto Gr. "Brilliant like the spade." Egbert, English saint who patiently imposed the celebration of Easter in his land at the same time that the rest of the Western Church did it. Remembered on April 24. Egbert, ninth-century Anglo-Saxon king.
(Egbert)

Egidio Gr. "Natural of Egeo." Religious man Egidio María de San José from Taranto, Italy, remembered on February 7.

Eladio Gr. "The Greek." Bishop of Toledo, Spain, remembered on February 18.

Elbio Celt. (masc. **Elba**) "Tall."

Eleázar Heb. "God is my help." In the Bible, son of Aaron who entered the promised land with Joshua. Two martyrs remembered on September 27 and August 1.

Eleodoro Gr. "Gift of the sun." Var. of ancient Helidoro.

Elián Lat. "Pertaining to the plebeian Roman family, Aelia."
Eliano

Elías Heb. "My God is Jehova." Hebrew prophet whose history is told in the book of the kings. St.

Elijah, patriarch of Jerusalem, remembered on July 20.
(Eli or Elias)

Eliécer Heb. "God is my help." Eleven biblical characters, the most famous of whom is the servant of Abraham, sent by him to find a wife for his son Isaac.
Eliézer (Eleazer)

Elio Gr. "Sun." Var. **Elián**.

Eliseo Heb. "God is my salvation." Hebrew prophet, disciple of Elijah. Cuban poet Eliseo Diego.

Eloy Lat. "The chosen." French form of **Eligio**, more commonly used now. St. Eloi, bishop of Noyon, considered the patron of watchmakers, remembered on December 1. Venezuelan poet Eloy Escobar (1829–89).

Emanuel Heb. "God is with us." Original form of **Manuel**. Mexican singer Emmanuel.

Emérito Lat. Ancient Roman soldier rewarded for his successes. Saint, martyr, remembered on February 11.

Emiliano Lat. Var. **Emilio**. Saint, martyr, remembered on December 6. Mexican revolutionary leader Emiliano Zapata.
(Emil)

Emilio Lat. Pertaining to the renowned family of the Roman nobility, the Aemilia. Saint, martyr remembered on May 22. *Émile*, novel by Rousseau. Music producer Emilio Estéfan.

Eneas Gr. "Worthy of praise." In mythology, Aeneas, son of Anchises and Aphrodite, hero in Homer's *Iliad*. Trojan prince, whom Virgil made a hero in his epic poem the *Aeneid*.

Enio Gr. "The ninth son." Roman epic poet from the second century B.C.

Enoc Heb. "Devoted to God." In the Bible, Enoch, seventh patriarch after Adam and father of Methuselah.
(Enoch)

Enrique Ger. "Prince of his land." St. Henry the emperor who governed Germany under the name of Henry II and later was emperor of Rome, remembered on July 15. Shakespeare's *Henry IV* (Parts 1 and 2), and *Henry V*. Many kings of England, France, and Spain. Puerto Rican author Enrique Laguerre.
Quique, Enriquillo (Henry)

Enriquillo Sp. Der. **Enrique**. Indian chief from the Dominican Republic who fought against the Spaniards until 1533 when he obtained freedom for all the Indians on the island. Historic novel by Dominican Manuel de Jesús Galván.

Enzo It. Short for **Vicenzo** and **Lorenzo,** now used as a name in itself. Italian designer Enzo.

Epifanio Gr. "The one who gives light." St. Epifanio, bishop of Salamina, remembered on May 12.
(Epiphany)

Erasmo Gr. "Amicable, desirable." Desiderius Erasmus, sixteenth-century Dutch scholar who attempted to solve some of the controversies of the time of the Reformation. Saint, martyr, remembered on June 2.
(Erasmus)

Erberto Ger. "Brilliant warrior." Saint, bishop of Toulouse, remembered on May 14, also known as Eremberto.
(Herbert)

Erico Ger. "Honorable prince." Fourteen kings of Denmark, Sweden and Norway. Saint, martyr, Erico of Sweden, remembered on May 18.
Eric, Erik

Ermindo Ger. Var. **Armando.** "The warrior."

Ernesto Ger. "Severe, decisive." A king of Hanover, two English dukes, an archduke of Austria, and various princes. Characters in José Echegaray's *El gran galeoto* and Oscar Wilde's *The Importance of Being Earnest*. Argentine writer, Ernesto Sábato. Mexican President Ernesto Zedillo. Cuban composer Ernesto Leowona.
(Ernest or Ernie)

Eros Gr. "God of love."

Ervino Ger. "Friend of the honors." Translation of the German Erwin, from architect Erwin Steinbach, who built the beautiful cathedral of Strasbourg.
(Ervin, Erwin)

Esaú Heb. "Of long hair; hairy." In the Bible, first son of Isaac and Rebecca, brother of Jacob, to whom he sold his primogeniture and was therefore disinherited.

Escolástico Lat. "Well-educated."

Estanislao Slavic. "Glory of their homeland." Two saints, one bishop of Cracow, the other young Jesuit of Kostka, Poland, remembered on April 11 and November 13, respectively.

Esteban Gr. "Crown of victory." Many saints and martyrs, among them, Pope Stephen I and St. Stephen, king of Hungary, remembered on August 2 and September 2, respectively. Also the first martyr St. Stephen, whose life is chronicled in the Acts of the Apostles. Argentine writer Esteban Echeverría (1805–51).
(Stephen or Steven)

Estrellita Lat. Uncommonly used as a boy's name. Argentine writer and professor Estrella Gutiérrez.

Euclides Greek mathematician.

Eudosio Gr. (masc. **Eudosia**) "Well thought of."

Eufemio Ger. (masc. **Eufemia**) "One who says good words."

Eugenio Gr. "Well born." St. Eugenius I, seventh-century pope, remembered on June 2. Also Popes Eugenius II, III, and IV. Nineteenth-century Puerto Rican educator and publicist Eugenio María Hostos.
(Eugene or Gene)

Eulalio Gr. (masc. **Eulalia**) "One who speaks well."

Eulogio Gr. "Good at reasoning." St. Eulogio of Córdoba, archbishop of Toledo, Spain, and martyr of the Muslims, remembered on March 11.

Eurípides Gr. Greek tragic playwright.

Eusebio Gr. "Pious." Various saints and martyrs, among them St. Eusebius, bishop of Vercelli, remembered on August 2.

Eustacio Gr. "Of good and great firmness." Two saints, martyrs: Eustacio White, remembered among the London martyrs of 1951, and St. Eustacio, remembered on December 10 and April 14, respectively.

Eustaquio Gr. "Tall." St. Eustaquio of Antioch, wise and eloquent man, remembered on July 16.

Evangelista Gr. Each of the four sacred writers who wrote the gospel. People assigned to sing the gospel in the church. St. Juan the Evangelist, remembered on November 27.

Evaristo Gr. "Excellent or very agreeable." Saint, pope from Rome, remembered on October 26.

Everardo Ger. "Strong like a wild boar." Religious man, abbot of Marchthad, remembered on April 17.

Exequiel Heb. "God is my strength." In the Bible, the third of the four greater prophets who lived in exile in Babylonia.

Ezequiel (Ezekiel)

Ezequías Heb. "My strength comes from God." Thirteenth king of Judah whose story is told in the Book of Kings and who did what was good in the eyes of God.

F

Fabián Lat. "Son of Fabio, descendant of the noble Roman family of the same name." Saint, pope, and martyr in the year 236, remembered on January 20.

Fabio Lat. "Pertaining to the Fabia family." Various illustrious Roman generals. Ancient Latin historian Fabio Pictor. Model/spokesperson Fabio.

Fabricio Lat. "The artifice." Third-century Roman General Fabricio Cayo. Hero in French novelist and essayist Stendahl's novel, *The Charterhouse of Parma*.
(Fabrice)

Facundo Lat. "Eloquent." Spanish saint martyr, remembered on November 27. Historic Argentine character immortalized in Domingo Sarmiento's book *Facundo* or *Civilization and Barbarity*.

Faustino Der. Fausto. Faustinus, two saints and martyrs, remembered on February 15 and July 2.
(Faust)

Fausto Lat. "Happy, fortunate." Two saints, one bishop of Riez, born in Britain, and the other, martyr with St. Genaro and St. Marcial, who together comprise the "three crowns of Córdoba," in honor of the place in Spain where they jubilantly offered their lives and were thrown to the bonfire. Main character in Goethe's two-part drama of the same name, in which Faust sells his soul to Mephistopheles for knowledge and power. Argentine poem from Estanislao del Campo.

Federico Ger. "Peace lover." Saint and martyr Frederick of Utrecht and religious man Federico of Ratisbona, remembered on July 18 and 29, respectively. Three German emperors and various kings and princes of Prussia, Poland, and Sweden. Spanish poet Federico García Lorca. U.S. Secretary of Transportation Federico Peña.

Fedoro, Freddy (Frederick)

Fedor Rus. "Gift of God." Three Russian czars. Russian writer, Fyodor Dostoyevski.

(Fred)

Fedro Gr. "Splendid." Latin fable writer, freedman Caesar Augustus.

Feliciano Lat. Der. **Félix.** Two saints, martyrs, remembered on January 24 and June 19. Singer José Feliciano.

Chano

Felipe Gr. "Friend of the house." Philip, one of the twelve apostles, remembered on May 11. Many Christian saints and martyrs. Many kings of Spain, France, and Portugal. Franciscan saint and martyr Felipe de Jesús, born in Mexico and crucified in Nagasaki, Japan, remembered on February 5. Felipe de Borbón, Prince of Asturias, Spain, since 1977. Spanish Prime Minister Felipe González.

(Philip or Phillip)

Félix Lat. "Happy." Over twenty saints and martyrs, among them four popes, starting with Felix I, remembered on May 30.

Fénix Lat. "Symbol of immortality." In Egyptian mythology, the phoenix, a beautiful bird that lives in Arabian desert for five to six hundred years and then sets itself on fire, rising renewed from the ashes to start another long life.
(Phoenix)

Fermín Lat. "Constant, firm." Saint and martyr, bishop of Pamplona, remembered on July 7 with the famous bull races on the streets of Pamplona. Character in Spanish writer Leopoldo Alas's (known as Clarín) novel *La Regenta*.
Fermino

Fernán Ger. Short for **Fernando**. Famous Castilian Count Fernán González, who fought and obtained independence for his land from the reign of León. Fernán Caballero, name with which Spanish novelist Cecilia Böhl de Faber signed her books.

Fernando Ger. "Audacious in peace." Various saints, among them St. Fernando III, king of Castile, who also defeated the Moors, remembered on May 30. Spain's kings Fernando I through VII. Also kings and emperors of Germany, Austria, Italy, and Portugal. Puerto Rican historian Francisco Picó. King Fernando II reigned when Christopher Columbus discovered America. Baseball player Fernando Valenzuela. Colombian painter and sculptor Fernando Botero.

Fidel Lat. "Loyal." Two saints and martyrs, St. Fidelis of Sigmaringen, killed for spreading the Catholic faith among the Calvinists, and St. Fidel of Como, remembered on April 24 and October 28, respectively. Cuban President Fidel Castro.

Filemón Gr. "Lover of good manners, affable." In mythology, Philemon, one of the Greek characters whose story is told in Ovid's *Metamorphosis*. Two martyrs, St. Filemón and St. Filemon, remembered on November 22 and March 8, respectively. Greek comic poet.

Filiberto Ger. "The one who has a lot of brightness." Saint, abbot born in Gascony, remembered on August 20.
(Philbert)

Flaviano Lat. Der. **Flavio**. Saint, martyr, patriarch of Constantinople in 447, remembered on February 18.

Flavio Lat. "Pertaining to the ancient Roman family, Flavia." A third-century B.C. Roman jurist.

Florencio Lat. "The one who has or gives flowers." Two saints and martyrs, St. Florencio, bishop of Strasbourg, and St. Florencio, remembered on November 7 and December 14, respectively.
(Florence)

Florentino Lat. "From Florence, Italy." Saint and martyr, remembered on October 10.

Florián Lat. Der. Flora, and used as its masc. Fourth-century saint and martyr known as protector against fire and water, remembered on May 4.

Florindo Lat. (masc. **Florinda**) Der. **Flora**. "Like a flower."

Fortunato Lat. "Fortunate, happy, prosperous." Various saints and martyrs. St. Fortunato of Hadrumentum, Africa, of the twelve Martyr Brothers, all remembered on September 1.

Francisco Ger. "The one with the lance." Various saints including St. Francis of Assisi, defender of the poor and founder of the Franciscan order, remembered on September 17. Spanish general and dictator Francisco Franco. Various kings and emperors in Europe. Mexican revolutionary Francisco "Pancho" Villa. Spanish conquistador Francisco Pizarro.

Chico, Fran, Francesco, Paco, Pacorro, Panchito, Pancho, Paquito (Francis or Frank)

Franco Ger. "From the Franks, German people who conquered and gave name to France." Spanish general and dictator Francisco Franco. Argentine poet Luis Franco, born in 1898. Paraguayan president Manuel Franco.

(Frank)

Froilán Ger. "Young gentleman." Ninth-century saint, Apostle of Spain, patron of the province of León, remembered on October 5.

Froylan

Fructuoso Lat. "Fruitful." St. Fructuosos, bishop and martyr of Tarragona, Spain, remembered on January 21, and archbishop of Braga, Portugal, remembered on April 16.

Fulgencio Lat. "Brilliant, resplendent." Saint, canon of Seville and bishop of Ecija, Spain, remembered on January 14. Cuban general and dictator Fulgencio Batista.

Fulvio Lat. (masc. **Fulvia**) "Reddish hair."

G

Gabino Lat. "From Gabio, Italy." Saint remembered on February 19.
Gaby

Gabriel Assyrian. "Man of God." Various saints and martyrs, but mainly St. Gabriel the Archangel, who announced to Virgin Mary that she had been chosen as the mother of God. Remembered on May 24. Colombian Nobel Prize–winner Gabriel García Márquez. Cuban poet Gabriel de la Concepción Valdéz.

Galileo Heb. "From Galileo, Palestine." Italian astronomer, mathematician, and physicist who demonstrated the truth of the Copernican theory with the telescope. Condemned for heresy in the Inquisition.

Galindo Der. **Galo**. Bishop of Troyes, France, who wrote the historical annals of France.

Galo Lat. "From Galia, ancient name of France." A third-century Roman emperor. Gallo, two saints, one an Irish apostle of Switzerland, remembered on October 16, and the other the bishop of Clermont, remembered on July 1.

Gamal Arab. Probably short for **Gamaliel**, from Hebrew.

Gamaliel Heb. "God is my reward." Doctor of Letters, secret disciple of Jesus, and teacher of Saint Paul.

Garcilaso Comb. form **García** and **Laso.** Spanish poet Garcilaso de la Vega (1501–36). Peruvian historian Garcilaso de la Vega known as the Inca (1539–1616), son of a conquistador and an Incan princess.

Gaspar Per. "Guardian of the treasure." Caspar, one of the three kings who followed a star to the place where Jesus was born in Bethlehem, remembered on January 6. Mexican Indian writer Antonio Gaspar (died in 1583).

Gastón Ger. "The foreigner, the guest." From Gascony, region in the south of France. Saint, founder of the Order of St. Anthony, remembered on April 24.

Genciano Lat. "Born blue." Saint martyr, remembered on December 11.

Genaro Lat. "Born in the first month of the year, January." Various saints and martyrs, including St. Gennaro, bishop of Benevento, Italy whose old solidified blood is in a church in Naples, and three times a year it liquefies in front of the followers. Remembered on September 19.

Generoso Lat. "Noble and illustrious." Spanish word for generous.

Geraldo Ger. "The one who reigns with a lance." St. Gerald, count of Aurillac, France, and St. Geraldo of Saar, remembered on October 13 and April 19 respectively. TV talk show host Geraldo Rivera.
(Gerald)

Gerardo Ger. "Strong with the lance." A dozen saints and martyrs, among them St. Gerard, bishop of Csanad, originally from Venice, whose relics are in the Island of Murano, remembered on September 24. Pop star Gerardo.

Gerardito, Gerri, Gerry (Gerard)

Germán Ger. "Warrior man." Various saints, including St. German, patriarch of Constantinople, remembered on May 12, and St. Germanus, bishop of Auxerre, France, remembered on July 31. St. German, town in Puerto Rico.

Germano (Germain)

Gerónimo Gr. "Sacred name." Apache Indian chief.

Gervasio Gr. "The lance of power." St. Gervase, remembered on June 19.

(Gervase)

Gil Lat. For some, popular form of **Egidio.** Various saints, including St. Gil, Athenian abbot on whose life is based the famous medieval legend of a servant invulnerable to arrows, remembered on September 1. Main character in Spanish writer Tirso de Molina's *Don Gil de las calzas verdes*.

Gilberto Ger. "Distinguished by the lance." St. Gilbert, bishop of Caithness, Scotland, and St. Gilbert of Sempringham, founder of the Gilbertine Order, remembered on April 1 and February 4, respectively. Salsa singer Gilberto Santo Rosa.

(Gilbert)

Ginés Gr. "The one who engenders life." Saint, martyr Ginés the Comedian, remembered on August 25.

Glen Ir. Gael. "A narrow valley between hills." Puerto Rican singer Glen Monroigen.

Godofredo Ger. "Peace of God." French knight Godogredo of Bouillón, Duke of Lorena, who directed the first Crusade against the unfaithful. Various saints, among them, Godofredo of Amiens, bishop of great severity and justice, remembered on November 8.

(Godfrey, Godfried)

Gonzalo Ger. "Saved from combat." Devout Gonzalo de Amarante and martyr Gonzalo García, remembered on January 16 and February 5, respectively. Tennis star Pancho Gonzales.

González, Gonzo, Gonzolito

Gracián Lat. "Who possesses grace." Devout person, Gracián de Cattaro, remembered on November 16.

Graciano

Gregorio Lat. "The one who keeps guard." Name of ten saints and sixteen popes, among them St. Gregory I the Great, pope and Doctor of the Church who advanced the conversion of England, remembered on March 12.

Gergori, Gregorito (Gregory)

Grimaldo Ger. "Powerful protector." Saint remembered on September 29.

Gualberto Ger. "Brilliant in power." Saint, abbot of Florence, St. John Gualbert, founder of the Vallombrosian monks, remembered on July 12.

Guido Ger. "The man of the forest." Saint, abbot, Guido of Pomposa, remembered on March 31.

(Guy)

Guillermo Ger. "Protector of firm will." Many saints and martyrs, including St. William, archbishop of York, remembered on June 8. Three emperors of Germany, various kings of England, Holland, Belgium, and Sicily. Cuban writer Guillermo Cabrera Infante. Cuban musician Willie Chirino.

(Guillaume)

Gumersindo Ger. "Excellent male." Saint, martyr,

Gumersindo of Córdoba, Spain, killed by the Arabs in the ninth century, remembered on January 13.

Gustavo Ger. "The one who possesses the noble scepter." Four kings of Sweden. Spanish nineteenth-century poet Gustavo Adolfo Bécquer.
(Gustave)

H

Habib Heb. "Beloved one."

Hakeem Arab. "Wise one."
Hakim

Hamlet O.G./Fr. "Village." Derived from the German root that means "home." Commonly associated with Shakespeare's troubled Danish prince.
Amlet, Amleto, Hamleto

Harmodio Gr. "Agreeable." Taken from the Greek words for "harmonious, happy, well-adjusted, and adaptable."
Armo, Harmo, Harmon, Harmonito

Heberto Fr. Der. **Herberto,** which referred to various German warriors.
Hebe, Berti, Bertito, Berto

Héctor Gr. "Holds firm." An illustrious hero of the Trojan war. Puerto Rican salsa singer Héctor Lavoe.

Heladio Gr. "Born Greek." The most Greek of names because it signifies Greekness. A bishop of Toledo bore this name. "Helado" is the Spanish word for "cold" as well as for "ice cream."
Eladio, Eladito, Heladi, Heladito, Helio

Heliodoro Gr. "From the sun." In the early centuries there were three martyrs who bore this name, including an Italian bishop. Greek novelist.

Elio, Helio, Heliodo, Helito, Lio, Liodo

Helvecio Lat. Helvetii, the ancient inhabitants of what is now Switzerland.

Helve, Helvi, Helvita, Veci, Vecito

Henrique Portuguese variation of **Enrique**.
(Henry)

Hércules Gr. "Glory of Hera." The Greek hero of incredible strength. Since his name also related to a person who defends property, it has been associated with the Spanish word herencia or "heritage."

Heraclido, Hercu, Hergelio

Heriberto Ger. "Bright warrior." Adopted by various religious and military leaders and used in several forms, depending on the country. The German and English form is Herbert; the Italians use Erberto.

Hermán Ger. "Army man." Often used with a G, as in Germán. Originally a Norman name.

Arman, Armando, Armín, Germán, Hariman, Harman, Hermano and Hermanito (brother, little brother), Herminio

Hermes Gr. "Messenger." The messenger of the gods whose name was taken by twenty-seven saints.

Ermes, Ermete, Ermito, Hermete, Hermeto, Hermilo, Herminio, Hermion, Hermito

Hernán Der. Hernando.

Hernando Sp. Var. **Fernando**. "Audacious in peace."

Hernan, Hernani, Hernanito

Hildeberto Ger. "Brilliant warrior." A popular soldier's name. Also St. Hildeberto of Fontenelle in France.

Hildebert, Ilbert (Hilbert)

Hillel Heb. "Praised." A common Jewish name that honors the first-century Jewish scholar Rabbi Hillel.

Hipócrates Gr. "A horseman." The name of the most famed doctor of ancient times.

Hiram Heb. "Noble." An Old Testament name. Hiram Bingham, the explorer who discovered the ruins of Machu Picchu in Peru and other famed archeological sites.

Homero Gr. "Security." Homer, the classical poet who wrote the *Iliad* and the *Odyssey*.

Homerico, Omero (Homer)

Honesto Lat. "Honest." The Spanish word for "dependable" or "honest."

Honoria, Honorato

Huáscar Quechua. "Gold chain." The surname of Inti Cusi Hualpa, brother of Atahualpa, the last Inca king. From the Quechua words for "rope" and "chain," alluding to the gold chain worn to celebrate the birth of the famous Inca Huayna Capac. Used almost exclusively in Peru and surrounding countries where the Incas lived.

Hugo Ger. "Clear intellect." A name from the Middle Ages that spawned many derivatives. French duke Hugo the Great. Mexican soccer star Hugo Sánchez. Peruvian soccer star Hugo Sotil, "El Cholo." French writer Victor Hugo.

Hewe, Hugh, Hugin, Hugolino, Hugón, Hugues, Huguito, Ugo, Ugone, Ugolino, Uguecria (Hugh or Hugo)

Humberto Ger. "Hun." Humbert Humbert, narrator of Vladimir Nabokov's *Lolita*. Italian author Umberto Eco.
Humbalda, Hunfredo, Hunfrido (Humbert)

I

Ignacio Lat. "Burning." Many Christian figures, especially St. Ignatius of Loyola, founder of the Jesuits.
(**Ignatius**)
Igor Rus. "Soldier." Composer Igor Stravinsky.
Ilario It. Var. **Hilary.**
Ilias Gr. Var. **Elijah.**
Ilidio Lat. "Belongs to the troops."
Inocencio Sp. "Innocent."
Irenio Gr. (masc. **Irene**) "Peace."
Isaac Heb. "Laughter." Born to Abraham when he was one hundred years old.
Isidoro Gr. (masc. **Isidora**) "Gift of Isis." St. Isidoro of Sevilla, doctor of the Church, is remembered April 14.
Israel Heb. "He who dominated God." This was the name given to Jacob in the Old Testament.
Italo Lat. "Italian."
Ivan Rus. Var. **Juan.** "God is beneficent."
Ivor Norse. Var. **Ivo.** "Yew wood."

J

Jacinto Gr. A mythological person that Apollo turned into a flower by metamorphosis.
(Hyacinth)

Jacobo Heb. Jacob, in the Old Testament, impersonates his hairy brother Esau by covering his hands with goatskin to secure the blessing of his blind father. Jacobo Morales, a Puerto Rican film director and Jacobo Timmerman, an Argentine human rights worker and journalist.
Giacobo, Giacomo, Iacovo, Iakob, Jackie, Jacomé, Jacques, Jakob, Jakov

Jacques Fr. Var. **James.** Two New Testament saints are named James. In Old Testament usually called Jacob.

Jaime Sp. James is the English version of Jacob. Actor Jaime Escalante.
(James)

Jalil Arab. Var. **Khalil.** "Friend."

Jasón Gr. Var. **Joshua.** "He will be healed." A legendary Greek hero who recovered the Golden Fleece from the enemy.

Javier Basque. "New house." St. Francis Xavier, a sixteenth-century Jesuit.
(Xavier)

Jenaro Lat. "January." Name of several saints, in-

165

cluding the Italian St. Gennaro, the bishop of Benevento.

Jeremías Heb. "Exalted by Yahiveh." Jeremiah, a prophet from the seventh century B.C.
Gerencia (Jeremy or Jeremiah)

Jerómino Gr. "Sacred." Geronimo, a famous Native American Apache. St. Jerome, an author of the Latin version of the Old Testament.
(Geronimo or Jerome)

Jeroteo Gr. "Consecrated by God." The first bishop of Athens.

Jesús Heb. Der. **Josú (Joshua)** used frequently in Latin America. The son of God in Christianity. Mexicans use Chucho or Chuy; Chileans use Jecho.
Jesulito, Josú, Josue

Jiméno Heb. Var. **Simeón** or the French **Chiméne**. "The one who listens."

Joaquín Heb. "God will be the judge." The father of the Virgin Mary. The Mexicans use **Guacho** while the French, English, and Germans use **Joachin**.
(Joachim)

Joel Heb. "Jehovah is God. " The most mentioned Old Testament prophet.
Joelo

Jonás Gr. A Greek version of Jonah, the biblical figure who survived being swallowed by a whale.
Jonaso (Jonah or Jonas)

Jonatán Der. **Nataniel** or **Natán**. Heb. "Gift of God." In the Old Testament, a friend of David.
Jon, John, Johnny, Natán, Nathaniel (Jonathan)

Jordán Heb. "Descendant." The river Jordan, where Jesus was baptized.

Jorge Gr. "Earth." A popular Latin American name that derives its appeal partly from its association to George in English, Georgius in Latin, Giorgio in Italian, and others. Mexican singer and actor Jorge Negrete. Argentine poet and writer Jorge Luis Borges.

Jorgito (George)

José Heb. "God increases." Joseph, an Old and a New Testament figure . New York congressman José Serrano. Venezuelan writer José Antonío Echeverría. Puerto Rican boxer José Chequi Torres. Singer José José. Chilean author José Donoso. Baseball player José Conseco. Cuban poet Jose Maria Heredia. Cuban writer José Lezana Lima. Spanish opera singer José Carreras. Venezuelan singer José Luis Rodriguez. Mexican singer José Mojica. Uruguayan writer José Enrique Rodó. Cuban liberator José Martí.

Che, Chiapaneco, Coche (Chilean), Geppe, Geppetto, Joseito, Joselito, Joselo, Pepe, Pepito, Peppe, Peppino (Joseph, Josh)

Joshé Heb. "God saves." The man who slowed down the sun.

(Josh or Joshua)

Jovino Lat. Der. **Jupiter.**

Javito (Jupiter)

Juan Heb. "God is beneficent." Probably the most common male name. John the Baptist. Juan de Oñate, founder of first colony in what is now the southwest United States, Juan Carlos I, current king of Spain.

Ivan, Jan, Jon, Juano, Juanito, Nanni, Niño (John)

Judas Heb. The traitor Apostle.

(Judas or Jude)

Julio Lat. Var. **Julias.** Singer Julio Iglesias. Boxer

Julio César Chávez. Roman Emperor Julius Caesar. Argentine writer Julio Cortázar. Dominican impersonator Julio Zabala.
Julian, Juliano, Julias, Julietto

Justino Lat. St. Justin, one of the founding fathers of the Latin church. Justino Díaz, an opera singer.
Justito, Justo, Jutto (Justin)

Juvenal Lat. "Juvenile."
Juvencio, Juvenciolo, Juventino

K

Kaled Arab. "Immortal." Used sporadically in the U.S. and adopted from the Syrian and Lebanese.
Kahlil, Kalil, Kalel, Khalil
Kim Eng. Taken from the English Kimberly.
Klaus Gr. Dim. **Nicholas**. "Leader in victory." Also spelled with a C.

L

Labán Heb. "Blanco." Name of a Hebrew patrician.
Lamberto Ger. "Brightest of the land."
Largo Lat. "Large." The Spanish word for "long."
Latino Lat. Someone who is Latin or Hispanic.
Laureano Lat. "Laurel."
   Laurencio, Laurentino, Lauro
Lautaro Araucano. A hero of the Chilean independence movement who died fighting the Spaniards in 1557. Used there and in Argentina.
   Lauro, Lautauro, Lauto (Larry)
Lázano Latin form of **Eleázar**, referring to a saint resuscitated by Jesus.
   Laza, Lazar, Lazarito (Lazarus)
Leandro Gr. "Lion man." Leander, the tragic lover of Hero in mythology.
Lemuel Heb. "Devoted to God." Name given by Swift to his hero Gulliver.
   Lemi, Muello
Lenin Rus. The revolutionary and statesman from Russia.
Leo Latin form of **León**, "the lion."
León Gr. "Lion."
Leonardo Gr. "Tough lion." From Lion but most

associated with Leonardo da Vinci. Also a saint from the Middle Ages.

(Leonard)

Leopardo Lat. "Leopard."

Leopoldo Ger. "The people." The name signifies "being bold among the people."

(Leopold)

Leví Heb. "Uniter." The name refers to a mother's hope that the birth of her son will unite her more to her husband. Also the third son of Jacob.

Liberato Lat. "Liberator." He who is free or liberated.

Libarado, Libario, Liberio, Libertad, Librado, Libro

Licio Gr. (fem. **Lidia**) "Light." Comes from Licia, the nickname given Diana, Apollo's lover.

Lino Gr. Linus, Apollo's son, who invented melody.

Lisandro Gr. "Liberator of men." A Trojan warrior from mythology.

Lobo Sp. The Spanish word for wolf.

Lorenzo Lat. An evolution of **Laurencio,** whose name was chosen because he was born beneath a laurel.

Larry, Lencho, Loreno, Lorent, Lorento, Loreto, Lorenzo, Nancio, Nenzio, Nenzo (Lawrence)

Lucano Lat. A region of Italy originally, but it also refers to light or luster.

Lucio, Luz, Luzano (Lucious)

Lucas Gr. or Lat. Luke, an evangelist who befriended St. Paul.

Luc, Luca, Lucelio, Lukas (Luke)

Lucero Lat. The planet Venus, also called Lucifer, which brings light to the morning.

Luz, Luzero

Luciano Lat. A popular religious name because it was used by several saints and martyrs.

Lucifer Lat. "He who brings light." A rebel angel who some believe is the devil.

Lucio Lat. "Light." A name given to those born at daylight.
(Lucius)

Ludovico Lat. Var. **Luis**. "Warrior."
Lodoris, Lodovico, Ludovick, Ludovic, Ludovie
(Ludwig)

Luis Gr. Fr. "Warrior." A form of Ludwig used by eighteen French kings. The British use Lewis and Louis. Mexican singer Luis Miguel. U.S. Congressman Luis Gutiérrez. Venezuelan singer José Luis Rodríguez. Puerto Rican statesman Luis Ferré. Author Louis L'Amour.
Lewis, Lodorico, Lovie, Lucho, Ludovico, Ludovicus, Luduig, Ludvik, Ludwig, Luigi (Louis)

Lutero A German last name used to demonstrate devotion to Protestantism.
(Luther)

M

Macario Gr. "Happy, blessed." Various saints, among them St. Macario of Jerusalem who was present when the Holy Cross was discovered, remembered on March 10. Also the Spanish St. Macario, who was martyred in Sevilla.

Macedonio Gr. "From Macedonia."

Magín Lat. "He who has imagination." Spanish hermit, remembered on August 25.

Magdal, Magi, Magus

Magno Lat. "The great." Two martyrs, St. Magnus, deacon of Pope Sixtus II and St. Magnus of Orkney, remembered on August 6 and April 16, respectively.

Malco Heb. "Like an angel." Spanish form of Malel. In the Bible, servant of Caiaphas who got an ear cut by Peter the Apostle, and Jesus restored it. Two saints, remembered on October 21 and July 27.

Mamerto Lat. "From Momertium, Italy." St. Memerto, bishop of Viennes, France, remembered on May 11. Argentine prelate and writer Brother Mamerto of Esquiér of the Franciscan Order.

Manfredo Ger. "Man of peace." King of Sicily, son of Emperor Federico II, made popular by literature. Main character in Byron's drama *Manfred*.
(Manfred)

Manuel Heb. Dim. **Emanuel**. "God is with us." Emmanuel, name the prophets gave to the Messiah who was coming to live with mankind. Puerto Rican writer Manuel Ramos Otero. Former Panamanian dictator Manuel Noriega. Former U.S. Secretary of the Interior Manuel Luján. Spanish bullfighter Manolete. Spanish singer Joan Manuel Serrat.
Mano, Manolo, Manuelito

Marcelino Lat. Dim. **Marcelo**. Various saints and martyrs, among them St. Marcelino, bishop of Embrum. African priest remembered on April 20 and devout man Marcelino Champgnat, founder of the Marist Brothers Institute, remembered on June 6.
Marcel (Marcellino)

Marcelo Lat. Dim. **Marcos**. Various saints and martyrs, among them two popes. St. Marcelus I, remembered on January 16 and St. Marcel II, who died twenty-one days after his election. Italian actor Marcello Mastroianni.
Marcel (Marcel)

Marcio Lat. "Born in March (Marzo) or consecrated to the god Marte." Saint, abbot of Clermond, remembered on April 13.
Marcial

Marcos Lat. Probably from an Arian root that means "to break." Various saints and martyrs, among them St. Mark, the second of the Evangelists, disciple of St. Peter who founded the

Church of Alexandria, remembered on April 25. Main character in Vicente Espinel's *Marcos de Obregón* and spiritual son of *Lazarillo de Tormes*. Singer Marco Antonio Muñiz.
Marc (Marcus)

María Heb. Commonly used in the past as a male name preceded by a male name, such as José María.
(Mary or Maria)

Mariano Lat. "Devoted or pertaining to the Virgin Mary." Various saints and martyrs, and a famous devout man Mariano Scotto, abbot, copier of religious texts, and founder of the first monastery for the Irish, remembered on February 9.
(Marion)

Marino Lat. "Man of the sea." Various saints, among them the founder of the hermitage of Mount Titano, where later a big monastery was built that marked the beginning of the capital of the republic of San Marino, remembered on September 4.

Mario Lat. Pertaining to the illustrious Roman family Maria, whose most probable meaning is "manly." For many, masc. **María.** Saint and martyr who was decapitated with his family by orders of Emperor Claudius in the second century because they devoted themselves to the ashes of their burned martyrs. Peruvian novelist Mario Vargas Llosa. Mexican comedian Mario Moreno, known as Cantinflas. Cuban musician Mario Bauzá. Main character in Walter H. Pater's *Marius the Epicurean*.
(Marius)

Marón Arab. "Male saint." Saint, abbot who lived alone in the city of Cirrus, Syria, whose disciples in Lebanon collected his relics and built a monastery over his tomb. They are called the Maronitas. His feast is celebrated on February 14. Also the Spanish word for "brown."

Martín Lat. Dim. **Martino.** "Born on Tuesday." Various saints, among them St. Martin of Tours, one of the most popular bishops of France, patron saint of Buenos Aires, Argentina, and religious man Martín de Porres, Dominican of Peru, remembered on November 11 and 5, respectively. Main character in Argentine writer José Hernández's epic gaucho poem, *Martín Fierro*.
(Martin)

Martino Lat. "Born on Tuesday (Martes)." Three popes of the church, one of them St. Martino I, martyr who suffered tremendously in jail and was exiled. Remembered on November 12.
Martiano, Martiniana (Martin)

Mateo Heb. "Devoted to God." Various saints and martyrs, among them St. Matthew the Apostle. The first of the four evangelists, remembered on September 21.

Matías Var. **Mateo.** Matthias, who accompanied Jesus from the baptism through the Ascension, becoming part of the twelve apostles when he was designated to replace Judas, remembered on February 24.
(Matthias or Matthew)

Mauricio Lat. Der. **Mauro.** Various saints and martyrs, among them St. Maurice, chief of the Theban Legion, killed with all his soldiers in

Martigny, Switzerland, for confessing his Christianity and refusing to persecute other Christians. Remembered on September 22.

Maurie, Moris (Maurice)

Mauro Lat. "Of brown skin and also Moorish, from Mauritania, Africa." St. Maurus, abbot, remembered on January 15.

Maximiano Lat. Der. **Máximo.** Roman emperor who died in the fourth century. Two saints and martyrs, one of them part of the group of the Seven Sleepers of Ephesus, resuscitated after two hundred years of sleep from God's mercy saving them from persecution from Emperor Decius, remembered on July 27.

Maximiliano Lat. Comb. form **Máximo** and **Emiliano.** Three Roman emperors and one Mexican. Two saint-martyrs, Maximilian, bishop of Lorch, and Maxmilian of Carthage, remembered on October 12 and March 12, respectively. Mexican emperor Maximiliano.

(Maximilian)

Maximino Lat. Der. **Maximiano.** Two saint-bishops, the first from Aix, France who was one of the twelve disciples who left for France after the Ascension, according to legend, and the second from Tréveris, Italy, remembered June 8 and May 29, respectively.

Máximo Lat. "The greatest." Three Roman emperors. Various saints and martyrs, among them Maximus the Confessor, abbot, one of the most distinguished theologians of the seventh century, remembered on August 13. Cuban liberator Máximo Gómez.

Medardo Eng. "Worthy of great honor." St. Médard, bishop of Vermandois, very popular among peasants in the north of France since the sixth century, protector of fields and vineyards, remembered on June 8.

Melanio Gr. "Black, dark-skinned." Saint, bishop of Reims, buried in Rennes, where his feast is celebrated on November 6.

Melchor Heb. "King of light." Melchior, one of the three kings that went to Bethlehem guided by a star to visit newborn Jesus, remembered on January 6, the Epiphany.

Melvin Possibly Gael., "polished chief," or OE. "sword friend."

Miguel Heb. "Who is like God." Chief of the celestial militia, St. Michael the Archangel, who defeated the dragon and whose apparition in the Gárgano Hill is remembered on May 8. Main character in Jules Verne's *Miguel Strogoff*. Mexican singer Luis Miguel. Guatemalan writer Miguel Ángel Asturias. Actor Miguel Ferrer. Spanish writer Miguel de Unamuno. Spanish writer Miguel de Cervantes Saavedra, author of *Don Quijote*.

Milton Eng. "Mill town." English poet who, after becoming blind, wrote *Paradise Lost*. Brazilian singer Milton Nacimiento.

Millán Lat. Var. **Emiliano.** Spanish saint Millán of Cogolla, abbot, famous for the monastery that today has his name, remembered on November 12.

Modesto Lat. "Honest, moderate." Various saints, among them St. Modesto, who undertook the moral and material reconstruction of the Holy Land, remembered on December 17.

Moisés Egypt. "Saved from the water." In the Bible, infant Moses is sent downriver in a basket and saved by the pharaoh's daughter to later become the leader of the exiled Israelites.
(Moses)

Mustafá Turkish. "The chosen." Name of various Sultans and Ottoman writers.

N

Nabor Heb. "Purity." Someone who is honorable and sincere. A knight of the Round Table.

Nadir Heb. "Opponent." A proper name only in Latin America.

Napoleón Heb. "Lion of Naples." Napoléon Bonaparte of Corsica.
León, Napoleone, Napolo

Narciso Gr. A mythological person in love with himself.
Narses (Narcissus)

Natal Lat. Refers to the Nativity of Jesus Christ.
Natalico, Natalio (Nathan)

Natanael Heb. "God has given." Jesus said he was a real Israelite who was never guilty of deception.
Nacho, Nata, Natán (Nathaniel)

Nazareno Heb. "From Nazereth." Jesus spent his youth in Nazareth, from where Joseph and Mary came.
Nazar, Názaro (Nazereth)

Nazario Heb. "Flower." In older Hebrew law a *Nazer* was a type of mystical initiation.
Nazairo, Nazaret, Nazareus, Názaro (Nazerus)

Neftali Heb. "Fight." Rachel, seeing that she was bearing no children for Jacob, offered to let her servant Bila bear his children. The first son was named Neftali.

Nelson Eng. "Son of Neil." Variation **Nigel**. Another Latinization is Nigelus, a diminutive of Niger, meaning "black," affectionately.

(Neil or Nelson)

Nereo Gr. "Swimmer." God of the sea.

(Nero)

Nestor Gr. "He who remembers." A mythological person who was one of the brightest generals of the Trojan War. Cuban cameraman Nestor Almendros.

Nesto, Nestorito (Nester)

Nicolás Gr. "Leader of the victory." Frequently adopted by religious leaders, it has become popular in Latin America because of St. Nicholas. Cuban poet Nicolás Guillén.

Nick, Nicky, Nicodemo, Nicomedes (Nicholas)

Nino Sp. "Little boy." Der. **Antonino** or **Antonio**.

Noél Fr. A French equivalent of the Spanish **Natalio**, which is used by Hispanics only because of its connection to Christmas.

Norberto Ger. "Renowned northerner."

Bert, Bertio, Berto, Nolberto (Norbert)

Norman OE. "Northerner." The Normans of France were from Scandinavia.

Normano, Normen, Normeno (Normen)

Nuncio It. "Messenger." From the word that gave us "announced."

Nunzio

O

Octavio Lat. "The eighth son of a family." Roman patrician family called Octavia. Saint, martyr remembered on September 22. Main character in Stendhal's *Armancia*. Mexican poet Octavio Paz.
Octaviano, Octavo (Octavious)

Oderico Ger. "Rich in properties."

Odilio or Odilón Ger. "Owner of enormous wealth." St. Odilón, abbott of the Cistercience convent of Clung, remembered on January 1.
Otildio

Odón Ger. Var. **Otón**. "Dominator." Various saints and devout persons, among them, Saint Odón the Good One, Archbishop of Canterbury, remembered on July 4.

Olaf Ger. "The glorious one." Saint, martyr considered patron and national hero of Norway, whose tombstone sprouted a fountain of miraculous water where later a sanctuary was built and converted into an important center of pilgrimage during the Middle Ages, remembered on July 29.
(Olav)

Olimpo or Olimpio Gr. Born or pertaining to the Olympus, a Greek mountain considered the home of the gods.

Olindo Prob. from Gr. "From Olinda, Greek colony." Character in Torguato Tasso's *Jerusalem Liberated*.

Oliverio Lat. "Coming from Olivia, or he who brings peace." One of the twelve knights of Charlemagne. Martyr, remembered on June 11.
Olivero (Oliver)

Omar Arab. "Who has a long life." Two Mohammedan caliphs and an Arab chief of Malaga. Last sovereign of Taifa who reigned in Badajoz, Spain in the 11th century.

Onofre Ger. "Defender of peace." Saint, hermit of Egyptian deserts, remembered on June 12.

Orestes Gr. "Mountainous." In mythology, son of Agamemnon and brother of Electra, with whose help he murdered his mother (to avenge his father, whom she had murdered). Armenian saint and martyr, remembered on December 13.
Oreste

Orlando Ger. "Equivalent to Rolando." Man who comes from the glorious country. The most famous champion of Charlemagne, immortalized in Ariostso's poem *Orlando Furioso*.
Landi, Lando, Orlan, Orland, Orlandito, Roland, Rolando

Oscar Ger. "Divine spear." Two kings of Sweden and Norway. Oscar the Grouch on *Sesame Street*. Salsa singer Oscar de León. Designer Oscar de la Renta. Writer Oscar Hijuelos.
Oscarito, Osqui, Osquitar

Osiris Egypt. "With strong eyesight." In mythology, divine creator, beginning of good.

Osmán Arab. "Tender like a young pigeon."

Osmar Ger. "Brilliant like the glory of God."

Osvaldo Ger. "Having the power of the gods." Saint, king of Northumberland, England, remembered on August 5. One of the main characters in Madame de Staël's *Corina or Italy*.

Osval, Osvaldito, Waldo, Valdo (Oswald)

Otón Ger. "Powerful God." A Roman emperor, four emperors from the occident, and various kings of Germany. St. Odón, bishop of Bamberga, extraordinary preacher of the Pomerania, remembered on July 2.

Ovidio Lat. "Shepherd." Latin classical poet Ovid, exiled to Ponto for his romantic writings.

Oziel Heb. "Having the strength of God." Biblical figure, uncle of Moses and Aaron.

P

Pablo Lat. "Short." Over thirty saints, martyrs, and devout men, among them St. Paul, Apostle of the Gentiles, great preacher, author of the Letters to Saint Paul, which were incorporated to the celebration of Mass, remembered on June 29. Eight popes. Main character in Bernardino de Saint Pierre's *Pablo and Virginia*. Chilean poet Pablo Neruda. Spanish cellist Pablo Casals. Spanish painter Pablo Picasso. Cuban singer Pablo Milanés.
Pablito, Paolo, Polo (Paul)

Paco Ger. Short for **Francisco**. Fashion designer Paco Rabanne.
Paquito

Pacífico Lat. "Quiet, calm, with peace." St. Pacific of Severino and devout man Pacífico de Cerano, remembered, respectively, on September 24 and June 8.

Paladio Lat. "Protected by the goddess Pallas." St. Paladio, bishop, evangelist in the British Isles, where he built three churches, remembered on July 7.

Palomo (masc. **Paloma**) Spanish bullfighter Palomo Linares.

Párides Gr. "The best for helping." In mythology,

Paris, son of Priam who kidnapped Helen, starting the Trojan War.

(Paris)

Parmenio Gr. "Studious and constant." Variation of Parmérides, fourth-century Greek philosopher.

Pascual Lat. "Easter, referring to the Resurrection." Two popes, one of them St. Pascual I, who found the body of St. Cecilia and dedicated a church to her, remembered on February 11.

Pascasio, Pascuale, Pascualino (Pasqual or Pascal)

Pastor Lat. "Shepherd." Name that Jesus calls himself, "the good shepherd," and that now is used for the prelates who care for souls.

Patricio Lat. "Of noble race." Various saints among them Saint Patricio of Armagh, apostle and patron of Ireland, remembered on March 17 with big celebrations.

Pat (Patrick)

Paulino Lat. "Devoted to Paul." Various saints, among them Saint Paul, bishop of York, considered the first apostle of the then most important kingdom of England, remembered on October 10.

Paulito

Paulo Lat. Variation of **Pablo**. Saint Paulo the Young One, from Salamis who was elected patriarch of Constantinople under the name of Paul IV, remembered on August 28.

(Paul)

Pedro Lat. "Stone of the Catholic church, name of the first pope." Long list of saints, martyrs and devout men, among them Saint Peter, Prince of the Apostles, brother of Andrew whose real name was Simon, but Jesus changed his name when he said "You are Peter and above this stone I will build my church," remembered on June 29. Governor of Puerto Rico Pedro Roselló. Mexican singer and actor Pedro Infante. Mexican singer Pedro Vargas. Spanish filmmaker Pedro Almodóvar. Puerto Rican revolutionary Pedro Albizo Campos. The Spanish translation of Fred Flintstone—Pedro Picapiedras.

Pedri, Pedrio, Pepe, Petrolino, Piero, Pietro (Peter)

Pelayo Gr. Spanish for **Pelagio**. "Marine." Founder of Spain's monarchy as the King of Asturias, after defeating the Moors.

Peregrino Lat. "Persons whose devotion leads them to visit sanctuaries." Saint hermit of Modena, Italy, remembered on August 1.

Perfecto Lat. "Perfect." Possessing a high degree of Christian virtue. Second-century saint and martyr from Córdoba, Spain, remembered on April 18.

(Perfect)

Pío Lat. "Devout, inclined to piety, pious." Twelve popes.

(Pious)

Pirro Gr. "The color of fire or ardor."

Plácido Lat. "Pleasing, gentle, serene." St. Plácido, abbott, remembered on June 12. Opera star Plácido Domingo.

(Placid)

Plato Gr. "Broad-shouldered." In Spanish it also means "plate." Greek philosopher Plato.

Platon

Pompeyo Gr. "The fifth son after the first." Famous Roman general, saint, martyr of Carthage, remembered on April 10.

Pompi, Pompilio, Pomponio (Pompei)

Ponce Gr. "Fifth." Made famous by Spanish explorer Juan Ponce de León. City in Puerto Rico.

Poncio Gr. "From the sea." Two saints, remembered on March 8 and May 14.
Ponciano

Porcio Lat. Pertaining to the Roman family named Porcio (seller or caretaker of pigs). Roman writer.

Porfirio Gr. "Dressed in purple." Various saints, among them St. Porfirio of Gaza, where he destroyed pagan temples. Character in Dostoyevski's *Crime and Punishment*. Mexican leader Porfirio Díaz.

Primitivo Lat. "The first one." Two martyrs, remembered on July 18 and June 10.
(Primitive)

Primo Lat. "The first born." Saint, martyr from Zaragoza, Spain, remembered on June 9. Spanish for "cousin."
Primito

Próspero Lat. "The fortunate one." Literally means "prosperous." Main character in Shakespeare's *The Tempest*.
(Prosper)

Prudencio Lat. "He labors with sensitivity and reserve."
Prudo, Prudón (Prudence)

Publio Lat. "From the pueblo." Celebrated Latin poet Ovid, author of *Metamorphosis*.

Q

Quintin Lat. Var. Quinto.
   Quiliano, Quintiliano, Quintilio, Quintino (Quentin)
Quinto Lat. "The fifth child of the family."
Quirino Lat. Nickname given by the Romans to Mars, god of war.

R

Rabí Heb. "My teacher." In the Gospels, Jesus is frequently called Rabi. Used in the state of Jalisco, Mexico, as a Christian name.
(Rabbi)

Radamés Egypt. The son of King Tut, Ramses, "Son of Ra," another pharaoh. Also Radame's from the Verdi Opera *Aida*.

Rafael Heb. "God heals." One of the Bible's three archangels. Italian Renaissance painter, Raphael. Singer Rafael Martos. Puerto Rican composer Rafael Hernández. Rafael Hernandez Colón, former governor of Puerto Rico.
Rafa, Raffael, Raffaello, Raffallo (Ralph)

Raimundo Ger. "Protector of the divine word."
Ray, Raymund, Raymundo (Raymond or Ray)

Ramiro Ger. From the Visogoth Ranamers. A Spanish martyr of the sixth century.

Ramón Sp. A Catalan version of **Raimundo.** A Spanish religious figure of the eighth century. Very popular in Latin America. Puerto Rican Statesman Ramón Emeterio Betances. Ramon Navarro, a silent picture star.
(Raymond)

Randolfo Ger. "Shield-wolf." Celebrated English poet from the seventeenth century.
Randall, Randalo, Rando, Randolfito (Randolph)

Raúl "Wolf." The French form of Randolf, Raoul, which has been adopted to Raul. Former Argentine President Raúl Alfonsín. Brother of the Cuban president, Raúl Castro. Actor Raúl Julia.
(Ralph)

Reinaldo OE. Var. **Reginald.** "Counsel power."
Ray, Raynaldo, Rey, Reynaldo (Rinaldo)

Remedio Lat. "Medicine." In Spanish it literally means "cure" or "medicine." Remedios, a character in Gabriel García Márquez's *One Hundred Years of Solitude*.

Remo Lat. "Fast." One of the legendary twins who founded Rome.
(Remus)

Renán The last name of a French historian and philosopher of great renown.

Renato Lat. "Born again." A name of pagan origin.

René Fr. A French form of **Renato.**

Ricardo Ger. "Chief." Richard I and II, kings of England. Desi Arnaz TV character, Ricky Ricardo. Richard of the Shakespeare plays. Singer Ricardo Montaner. Actor Ricardo Montalbán.
Rick, Rickie, Ricky, Rico (Richard)

Rigoberto Ger. "Brilliant and powerful."
Bert, Rigo

Roberto Ger. "Bright fame." Senator Robert Kennedy. Brazilian singer Roberto Carlos. Puerto Rican baseball player Roberto Clemente.
**Beto, Bob, Bobby, Rob, Robby, Robiche, Robín
(Robert or Robin)**

Rocio Lat. "Mist." Spanish for "dew." It was used as an advocation for the Virgin Mary.
Rocí (Rosy)

Rodolfo Ger. "Wolf-fighter." An archbishop of Borges in France and a bishop of Gubia in Hungary.
Rudo, Rodulfo (Rudolph)

Rodrigo Ger. "Famed warrior." Rodrigo Díaz de Vivar, the legendary El Cid Campeador.
Drigo, Rodi, Rodito (Roger)

Rolando Ger. "Renowned land." From the French Roland, this has become a very popular Spanish name.
Lanny, Orlando, Roland, Rollo, Rolly, Roly (Roland)

Román Lat. "From Rome." A Roman soldier converted by St. Lorenzo and a French bishop ordained by St. Martin.
Romano, Romarico (Roman)

Romeo Lat. A version of Roma, but mostly known from Shakespeare's *Romeo and Juliet*.

Rómulo Lat. One of the twins who founded Rome. He later murdered the other, Remus, over where to place the city. Venezuelan writer Rómulo Galegos. Venezuelan leader Rómulo Betancourt.
(Romulus)

Rubén Heb. "Look, a son!" The translation for the words uttered by Leah when she had her first child by Jacob. Panamanian singer Rubén Blades. Nicaraguan writer Rubén Darío. Puerto Rican independence leader Rubén Barrios.
Reuben, Rube, Rúben, Rubi, Rudesindo (Rueven)

Rufino Lat. St. Rufino of Sevilla, a third-century

martyr. Rufino Tamayo, Mexican painter.
(Rufus)

Ruperto Ger. "The glow of fame." Var. **Roberto**.
(Rupert)

S

Sabino Lat. "From Sabino, Italy." Famous Roman jurist during the times of Tiberius.
Sabel, Sebelio

Salomón Heb. "Man who loves peace." In the Bible, the son of David and Betsabé who built the Jerusalem Temple, wrote numerous works of literature, and was the wise king of Israel.
Salmon, Salono, Sol, Solaman, Soloman

Salvador Lat. "Savior of humanity." Name given to Jesus for having saved humanity with the ultimate sacrifice of his life, remembered on August 6 or November 9, the day of the Ascension. Painter Salvador Dalí. Former Chilean president Salvador Allende.
(Salvatore)

Salvio Lat. (masc. **Salvia**) "Saved." Various saints, including St. Salvio, bishop of Albi and a bishop of Amiens, remembered on September 10 and January 16, respectively.

Samuel Heb. "God has heard me." In the Bible, Hebrew judge and prophet; two Old Testament books are named for him.
Sam, Sammy, Sammie, Samuelito

Sancho Lat. Var. **Santo**. "Saint." Three kings of Navarra, three of Castille, two from León, and one from Aragón, all in Spain. Don Quijote's companion, Sancho Panza, in Cervantes's novel.

Sandro It. Short for **Alessandro**. "He who shelters."
Sandito, Sando (Sandor)

Sansón Heb. "Small sun." In the Bible, the son of Hebrew judge, Manoa, known for his extraordinary strength. One of the most important secondary characters in *Don Quijote*, Sansón Carrasco.
(Samson)

Santiago Sp. "Saint James." **Jacob** or **Jacobo**. In Spanish became **Iago** and with the addition of Sant (short for saint) in the front produced Santiago. Patron saint of Spain and of Mendoza, Argentina, remembered on July 25.

Santos Lat. Persons that the church declares as saints and that are thereafter venerated as such.
Santito, Santo

Saúl Heb. "The desired, cherished one." In the Bible, first king of Israel.
Sol

Saulo Gr. "Tender, delicate." Original name of St. Paul the Apostle.

Sebastián Gr. "Worthy of veneration." St. Sebastian, Christian soldier who joined the Roman army to stop the persecution of Christians but was killed in a hail of arrows. A favorite of the master painters. He is the patron of soldiers, remembered on January 20. San Sebastián, Spanish city.
Bastian, Bastien, Sebastiano, Sebo

Segismundo Ger. "The victorious protector." A German emperor, three kings of Poland, and one of Sweden. St. Segismundo, king of Borgone, abbott. Founder of the convent of St. Maurice of Agaunum in the Swiss Canton of Valais. Central character in Spanish writer Calderón de la Barca's *La vida es sueño (Life Is a Dream)*.

Segundo Lat. "The second child." Main character in Argentine writer Ricardo Güiraldes's novel *Don Segundo Sombra*.

Selim Arab "The peaceful."

Sem Heb. "Fame, reputation." In the Bible, Genesis, son of Noah and brother of Cam and Jafet, who survives with them in the ark. His descendants are known as Semites.

Serafín Heb. "Noble princess and angels with wings." Blessed spirits that distinguish themselves by the constant love for the divine and the intense movement by which they elevate inferior spirits to God. The highest angels in heaven.
Serafino, Serafito (Seraphim)

Sergio Lat. "The one who protects and guards." Four popes shared this name. Designer Sergio Valente.
(Serge)

Servando Lat. "The one who guards and defends." Bishop, probably from Ireland, remembered on July 1.

Servio Lat. "Son of slaves." Roman king.

Severino Lat. Der. **Severo**. "Firm on justice."
(Severin)

Severo Lat. "Rigorous and punctual with his duties." St. Severe, bishop, patron of Erfurt, Germany, remembered on February 1.
(Severe)

Sidonio Lat. "From Sidon, Fenice." St. Sidonio of

Ireland, founder of the Reims monastery, remembered in France on November 14.

Sigfrido Ger. "The one who won peace." Hero in Wagner's opera that bears the same name. Swedish apostle and bishop, remembered on February 15.
(Siegfried)

Silvano Lat. "Who lives in the forest." In mythology, sort of demi-god of the forest, son of Fauno.
Silvino (Sylvan or Silvanus)

Silverio Lat. "Born in the forest." Pope, St. Silverio.

Silvestre Lat. "Raised in the forest, or naturally from the country."
Silvestro (Sylvester)

Silvino Lat. Var. **Silvano.** Bishop, probably from Toulouse, who spent all his personal fortune in saving the slaves from the barbarians and in charities, keeping a horse as his only possession, remembered on February 17.
(Silvanus)

Silvio Lat. "The man of the forest." In mythology, son of Eneas and Lavinia. All the kings of Alba. Cuban singer Silvio Rodríguez.

Simeón Heb. "The one who has listened." St. Simeon, bishop and martyr, cousin of Jesus, and one of those who received the Holy Spirit on Pentecost. Tortured and crucified, remembered on February 18.

Simón Gr. Prominent New Testament name, one of the twelve apostles. Latin American liberator Simón Bolívar.
(Simon)

Sinforoso Gr. "The one who comes with many talents." Saint, martyr of Gaeta, remembered on August 22.

Siro Lat. "From Syria." First-century Latin mime poet Publio Siro. Bishop of Pavia, Italy, of which he is the patron saint, remembered on December 9.

Sixto Lat. "Courteous and refined." Three popes. Means "the sixth" in Spanish.

Sofanór Gr. "Wise man."

T

Tadeo Heb. One of the twelve apostles, also St. Judas. Also from *The Great "Tudeo"* by Adam Mickienwicz.
(Thadeus)

Tatiano (masc. **Tatiana**) Saint and martyr of the church Tatiano Dulas.

Telémaco Gr. "Time for war." A mythological person who was the son of Ulysses and Penelope and played an important role in the *Odyssey*.
(Telemecus)

Telmo Heb. A derivative of St. Erasmus, which became **Eramo** then **Elamo** and **Elmo**. He used to be the patron saint of sailors.
(Elmo)

Teodoro Gr. "Son of God." Various saints and martyrs, including St. Theodore of Canterbury, celebrated September 19.
Teodor, Teodomido, Teodorico, Teodosio, Teoduldo, Teodulindo (Theodore)

Teodosio Gr. "He gives to God." Three Eastern emperors, including one who united the east and west of Rome.

Terencio Lat. Belonged to a Roman family from Tarento. A famed Latin poetic comedian from the second century, Terencio Afer.
Terence (Terrance)

Tiberio Lat. "Born next to the Tiber." A Roman emperor and a martyr.
(Tiberius)

Timoteo Gr. "Honors God." Various saints of the church, including a disciple of St. Paul, remembered on May 9.
Tim, Timito, Timmy, Timo (Timothy)

Tito Lat. A Roman emperor who defeated the Jews and destroyed Jerusalem. Also a Latin historian, born in Padua.

Tobias Heb. "God is my good." Two biblical figures from the tribe of Neftuli.
Tobi, Tobio (Toby)

Tolomeo Gr. "Strong in battle." Twelve pharaohs of Egypt bore this name. The most renowned astronomer of ancient times.

Tomás Syr. "Twin brother." A long list of religious figures bear this name, particularly the Apostle who doubted the resurrection of Christ. St. Thomas Aquinas is also noteworthy. Cuban filmmaker Tomás Gutierrez Alea.

Tranquilino Lat. "Serene or tranquil." Saint remembered July 6.
Tranquilo

Tristán Cel. A legendary person from medieval literature whose name was adopted for Wagner's opera *Tristan and Isolde*.

Tulio Lat. "Destined for glory." The third king of Rome, Tulio Hostilio. The father of Raome, orator, writer, and philosopher Marco Tulio Cicerón.

U

Ubaldo Ger. "Bold-spirited." St. Ubaldo, the most patient of all saints, remembered May 16.
Ubaldino

Ulises Lat. A mythological person who was Penelope's husband and was the hero of the Trojan War, whose travels were chronicled in the *Odyssey*.
(Ulysses)

Urbano Lat. "Urbane" or "an inhabitant of the city." Eight popes bear this name.

Urias Heb. "God is my light." A biblical person from the time of Jeremy.
Uri, Uriano, Uriel (Uri)

Urso Lat. "Bear." Venezuelan journalist Uslar Pietri.
Ursus, Uslar

V

Valdemar Ger. Name of various famed Danish kings.
Valde, Valdo, Waldo

Valentín Lat. "Force and valor." St. Valentine of the holiday is the best known of those who bear this name.
Vale, Valeno, Valentiniano, Valentino

Valerio Lat. "Healthy and robust." The best known of the saints of this name was from Zaragoza.

Venarrcio Lat. "Homebody."

Venerando Lat. "Venerated." Bishop of Clermont, remembered January 18.
Venerado

Vicente Lat. "He who overcomes." St. Vincent de Paul, remembered for founding an order, is the best known of various saints with this name.
(Vincent)

Victor Lat. "Victorious." Taken by various religious figures, including a famed African saint. Author Victor Hugo.
Victorino, Victuriano

Vidal Sp. The Spanish form of "vital."

Virginio Lat. (masc. **Virginia**) "Virginal."

Vito Lat. "Happy." Related to Guido.
Vidal, Vital

Vivaldo Ger. St. Vivaldo, who nursed another religious figure through leprosy.
(Vivaldi)

Viviano Cel. "The tiny." A legendary Roman hero.

Vladimiro Slavic. "Prince of peace." In Spanish it is usually spelled **Bladamiro**.
(Vladimir)

X

Xanto Gr. "Blond-haired."
Xavier Basque. Var. of **Javier**. "New house."
  Xavier

Z

Zabad Heb. "Precious gift." Two biblical figures.

Zacarias Heb. "God remembers." A minor biblical prophet who lived in the sixth century before Christ.
(Zachary)

Zenobio Uncertain origin. Some believe it's Greek and means "the force of Jupiter."

Zoilo Gr. "Has life." A Greek Sophist who was called the Flagellant of Homer.

III

Saints' Names by Day

Nombres de Santos por Día

Many parents wish to honor the saint or religious figure on whose day their child was born. The following is a list by month of saints and their days. Each name is followed by a notation for masculine (M) or feminine (F) and each name can be found in the main alphabetical listings of names.

JANUARY/ENERO

For a baby born in January: Jenara (F)

1: Claro (M)
   Odilón (M)

2: Basilio (M)

3: Bertilia (F)
   Genoveva (F)
   Antero (M)

6: Adoración (F)
   Altagracia (F)
   Gaspar (M)
   Melchor (M)

7: Alderico (M)

8: Apolinar (M)
   Atico (M)

10: Agatón (M)

11: Salvio (M)

12: Cesaria (F)
    Arcadio (M)

13: Berno (M)
    Gumersindo (M)

January / Enero

- **14:** Fulgencio (M)
- **15:** Mauro (M)
- **16:** Gonzalo (M)
  Marcelo (M)
- **17:** Alba (F)
- **18:** Venerando (M)
- **19:** Ábaco (M)
  Basiano (M)
- **20:** Fabián (M)
  Sebastián (M)
- **21:** Fructuoso (M)
- **24:** Paz (F)
  Bábilas (M)
  Feliciano (M)
- **25:** Elvira (F)
  Artemio (M)
- **26:** Baltilde (F)
  Batilde (F)
  Margarita (F)
  Paula (F)
  Alberico (M)
- **27:** Ángela (F)
- **28:** Amadeo (M)
- **31:** Marcela (F)
  Martina (F)
  Ciro (M)

FEBRUARY/FEBRERO

1: Brígida (F)
   Severo (M)

2: Aída (F)
   Candelaria (F)
   Ansaldo (M)

3: Belinda (F)

4: Gilberto (M)

5: Agueda (F)
   Dominica (F)
   Felipe (M)
   Gonzalo (M)

6: Amando (F)

7: Egidio (M)

9: Mariano (M)

10: Escolástica (F)

11: Emérito (M)
    Pascual (M)

12: Eulalia (F)
    Marina (F)
    Amadeo (M)

13: Arcángela (F)

14: Adolfo (M)
    Marón (M)

15: Georgina (F)
    Avito (M)
    Faustino (M)
    Sigfrido (M)

17: Ágata (F)
    Alejo (M)
    Augusto (M)
    Silvino (M)

18:	Artemia (F) Eladio (M) Flaviano (M) Simón (M)	24:	Matías (M)
		25:	Claudiano (M) Constancio (M)
19:	Álvaro (M) Gabino (M)	26:	Alejandro (M)
		27:	Baldomero (M)
20:	Cenobio (M)	29:	Ermelinda (F)
22:	Abimael (M)		

MARCH/MARZO

For a baby born during Holy Week
Good Friday: Angustias (F); Soledad (F)
Saturday: Soledad (F)
Easter Sunday: Pascua (F)

3: Balbino (M)
   Caledonio (M)

4: Casimiro (M)

6: Coleta (F)

7: Felícitas (F)

8: Filemón (M)
   Ponce (M)

10: Atalo (M)
    Macario (M)

11: Oria (F)
    Eulogia (M)

12: Gregorio (M)
    Maximiliano (M)

16: Dionio (M)

17: Gertrudis (F)
    Patricio (M)

18: Cirilio (M)
    Cristián (M)

24: Aldemar (M)

25: Anunciación (F)
    Dimas (F)
    María (F)
    Baroncio (M)

26: Cástulo (M)

30: Amadeo (M) 31: Balbina (F)
    Dodo (M)   Acacio (M)
                    Guido (M)

APRIL/ABRIL

1: Celso (M)
   Gilberto (M)

2: Teodosia (F)

4: Ciríaco (M)

6: Celestino (M)

9: Casilda (F)

11: Gema (F)
    Estanislao (M)

13: Marcio (M)

14: Eustacio (M)

15: César (M)

16: Fructuoso (M)
    Magno (M)

17: Aniceto (M)
    Everardo (M)

18: Apolonio (M)
    Perfecto (M)

19: Geraldo (M)

20: Adalgisa (F)
    Crisóforo (M)
    Marcelino (M)

21: Anselmo (M)

22: Agapito (M)

23: Adalberto (M)

24: Egberto (M)
    Fidel (M)
    Gastón (M)

25: Antonieta (F)
    Macedonio (M)
    Marcos (M)

April / Abril

26: Alda (F)
Valeria (F)
Aniano (M)

27: Zita (F)

28: Dídimo (M)

29: Cercira (F)

30: Catalina (F)
Aimón (M)
Arquibaldo (M)

MAY/MAYO

1: Amador (M)

2: Mafalda (F)
Atanasio (M)

4: Mónica (F)
Florián (M)

7: Domiciano (M)

8: Benedicto (M)
Miguel (M)

9: Timoteo (M)

10: Alfio (M)
Cataldo (M)

11: Felipe (M)
Mamerto (M)

12: Domitila (F)
Gema (F)
Epifanio (M)
Germán (M)

13: Fátima (F)

14: Erico (M)
Ponce (M)

15: Berta (F)

16: Brendano (M)
Ubaldo (M)

19: Alcuino (M)
Calócero (M)
Celestino (M)

20: Baudilio (M)
Bernardino (M)

21: Crispín (M)

22: Casto (M)
Emilio (M)

24: María (F)
Gabriel (M)

25: Adelmo (M)
    Cenobio (M)

27: Beda (M)

29: Teodosia (F)
    Maximino (M)

30: Félix (M)
    Fernando (M)

31: Cancio (M)

JUNE/JUNIO

For a baby born the third Sunday in June: Sorocco (M)

1: Alta (F)
 Baltasar (M)

2: Biblis (F)
 Mariana (F)
 Atalo (M)
 Erasmo (M)
 Eugenio (M)

3: Cecilio (M)

5: Bonifacio (M)

6: Clotide (F)
 Besarión (M)
 Claudio (M)
 Marcelino (M)

7: Alcibíades (M)

8: Guillermo (M)
 Maximino (M)
 Medardo (M)
 Pacífico (M)

9: Diana (F)
 Primo (M)

10: Margarita (F)
 Olivia (F)
 Amancio (M)
 Primitivo (M)

11: Bernabé (M)
 Oliverio (M)

12: Onofre (M)
 Plácido (M)

13: Antonio (M)

14: Digna (F)

June / Junio

- **15:** Alicia (F)
  Cástora (F)
  Germana (F)

- **16:** Amando (M)
  Aureliano (M)
  Aurelio (M)

- **17:** Avito (M)
  Besarión (M)

- **18:** Efrén (M)

- **19:** Basiano (M)
  Feliciano (M)
  Gervasio (M)

- **20:** Adalberto (M)

- **21:** Consuelo (F)
  Albino (M)

- **22:** Magdelena (F)
  Albán (M)
  Eberardo (M)

- **23:** Agripina (F)
  Audrey (F)
  Aristocles (M)

- **24:** Bautista (M)

- **25:** Adalberto (M)

- **27:** Devota (F)
  Cirilo (M)

- **29:** Ema (F)
  Casio (M)
  Pablo (M)
  Pedro (M)

JULY/JULIO

1: Galo (M)
   Servando (M)

2: Gracia (F)
   Sinforosa (F)
   Faustino (M)
   Otón (M)

3: Anatolio (M)

4: Odón (M)

5: Arcángel (M)

6: Dominica (F)
   Tranquilino (M)

7: Benedito (M)
   Fermín (M)
   Paladio (M)

8: Adrián (M)

9: Adolfina (F)

10: Amalia (F)
    Carmelo (M)

12: Gualberto (M)

13: Sara (F)
    Anacleto (M)

14: Buenaventura (M)
    Camilo (M)

15: Edith (F)
    Donaldo (M)
    Enrique (M)

16: Eustaquio (M)

17: Generosa (F)
    Mercelina (F)
    Alejo (M)

18: Arnolfo (M)
    Federico (M)
    Primitivo (M)

19: Áurea (F)
Estela (F)
Arsenio (M)

20: Salvadora (F)
Bulmarco (M)
Elías (M)

24: Cristina (F)

25: Cristóbal (M)
Santiago (M)

26: Ana (F)
Bartolomea (F)

27: Aurelio (M)
Malco (M)
Maximiano (M)

28: Argimiro (M)

29: Beatriz (F)
Marta (F)
Federico (M)
Olaf (M)

30: Esperanza (F)
Abadon (M)

31: Germán (M)

AUGUST/AGOSTO

**For a baby born in August:
Agustín (M); Augusto (M)**

1: Sofía (F)
Alfonso (M)
Eleázar (M)
Peregrino (M)

2: Esteban (M)
Eusebio (M)

4: Aritarco (M)
Domingo (M)

5: Aimón (M)
Ansaldo (M)
Osvaldo (M)

6: Magna (M)
Salvador (M)

7: Claudia (F)
Cayetano (M)

10: Filomela (F)

11: Clara (F)

13: Belarmino (M)
Casiano (M)
Máximo (M)

14: Eberado (M)

15: Piedad (F)
Alepio (M)

16: Asuncíon (F)

18: Elena (F)
Eliana (F)
María (F)

20: Amador (M)
Filberto (M)

August / Agosto

21: Gracia (F)

22: Sinforoso (M)

23: Dorina (F)

24: Bartolomé (M)

25: Ginés (M)
Magín (M)

26: Ceferino (M)

27: Cesarino (M)

28: Agustín (M)

29: Sabina (F)

SEPTEMBER/SEPTIEMBRE

For a fall baby: Anonna (F)

1: Fortunato (M)
   Gil (M)

2: Donoso (M)
   Esteban (M)

3: Febes (F)

4: Marino (M)

6: Emperatriz (F)
   Beltran (M)

8: Adela (F)
   Caridad (F)
   María (F)

10: Auberto (M)
    Salvio (M)

11: Teodora (F)

12: María (F)

13: Milagros (F)

14: Crescencio (M)

15: Angustias (F)
    Dolores (F)

16: Edita (F)
    Eufemia (F)
    Cipriano (M)
    Cornelio (M)

17: Ariadna (F)
    Francisco (M)

19: Genaro (M)
    Teodoro (M)

21: Ágata (F)
    Mateo (M)

September / Septiembre

- **22:** Candido (M)
  Mauricio (M)
  Octavio (M)

- **24:** Amparo (F)
  Mercedes (F)
  Casiodoro (M)
  Gerardo (M)
  Pacífico (M)

- **25:** Aurelia (F)

- **26:** Calistrato (M)
  Dalmacio (M)

- **27:** Cosme (M)
  Eleázar (M)

- **29:** Grimaldo (M)

OCTOBER/OCTOBRE

1: Ananías (F)

2: Ángel (M)
   Custodio (M)

3: Atilano (M)

6: Bruno (M)

7: Artaldo (M)

8: Demetrio (M)

9: Andrónico (M)
   Demetrio (M)

10: Casio (M)
    Florentino (M)
    Froilán (M)
    Paulino (M)

11: Zenaida (F)

12: Pilar (F)
    Maximiliano (M)

13: Eduardo (M)
    Geraldo (M)

14: Bucardo (M)
    Calixto (M)

15: Teresa (F)

16: Eduvigis (F)
    Beltrán (M)

19: Cleopatra (F)
    Aquilino (M)
    Eduino (M)

20: Bertilia (F)
    Artemio (M)

21: Celia (F)
    Malco (M)

22: Celina (F)
    Elodia (F)
    Abercio (M)
    Andrónico (M)
    Donato (M)

23: Alucio (M)

25: Daría (F)
    Engracia (F)
    Ananías (M)
    Baltasar (M)
    Crisanto (M)
    Crisóforo (M)

26: Evaristo (M)

28: Agostina (F)
    Amaranto (M)
    Fidel (M)
    Paulo (M)

30: Alonso (M)

NOVEMBER/NOVIEMBRE

1: Benigno (M)

4: Agrícola (M)
Carlos (M)
Claro (M)

5: Martín (M)

6: Augusto (M)
Melanio (M)

7: Benigno (M)
Florencio (M)

8: Castorio (M)
Godofredo (M)

9: Agripino (M)
Salvador (M)

10: Arclino (M)

11: Franco (M)
Martín (M)

12: Cristián (M)
Martino (M)
Millán (M)

13: Ado (M)
Arcadio (M)
Diego (M)
Estanislao (M)

14: Sidonio (M)

15: Alberto (M)
Desiderio (M)

16: Gertrudis (F)
Matilde (F)
Edmundo (M)
Gracián (M)

19: Barlaam (M)

22: Apia (F)
Cecilia (F)
Filemón (M)

November / Noviembre

23: Clemente (M)
24: Flora (F)
26: Belindo (M)
27: Facundo (M)
30: Andrés (M)

DECEMBER/DICIEMBRE

1: Eloy (M)

3: Diodoro (M)

4: Bárbara (F)
Anón (M)

5: Crispina (F)

6: Dátiva (F)
Dionisia (F)
Emiliano (M)

7: Ambrosio (M)

8: María (F)

9: Atanasia (F)
Siro (M)

10: Eulalia (F)
Auberto (M)
Brian (M)
Ciríneo (M)
Eustacio (M)

11: Elda (F)
Dámaso (M)
Daniel (M)
Grenciano (M)

13: Otilia (F)
Amado (M)
Orestes (M)

14: Cruz (F and M)
Florencio (M)

16: Adelaida (F)

17: Modesto (M)

19: Anastasio (M)

23: Dagoberto (M)

24: Adela (F)
Delfín (M)

26: Dionisio (M)

December / Diciembre

27: Fabiola (F)

30: Anisia (F)
Anisio (M)

31: Colomba/
Columba (F)
Melania (F)

Bibliography

Anastasi, Atilio. *Diccionario de Nombres Propios*. Buenos Aires: Editorial y Librería Goncourt, 1991.

Diccionario práctico de la lengua española. Barcelona: Ediciones Grijalbo, S.A., 1988.

Elenes, Xavier, *Cómo escoger el nombre de su bebé*. México: Edicomunicación, S. A., 1990.

García-Pelayo y Gross, Ramón, *Pequeño Larousse en color*. México: Ediciones Larousse, 1986.

Salazar G., Salvador. *Nombres para el bebé*. México: Editorial Diana, 1993.

Tibón, Gutierre. *Diccionario etimológico comparado de nombres propios de persona*. México: Fondo de Cultura Económica, 1986.

Utilísima. *¿Qué nombre le pondremos? Guía de nombres propios*. Buenos Aires: Ediciones Lidiun, 1993.

AND BABY MAKES THREE...
COMPREHENSIVE GUIDES BY
TRACIE HOTCHNER

CHILDBIRTH & MARRIAGE

The Transition to Parenthood
75201-8/$10.95 US/$12.95 CAN

PREGNANCY & CHILDBIRTH

Revised Edition
75946-2/$11.00 US/$13.00 CAN

THE PREGNANCY DIARY

76543-8/$11.00 US/$15.00 CAN

Buy these books at your local bookstore or use this coupon for ordering:

Mail to: Avon Books, Dept BP, Box 767, Rte 2, Dresden, TN 38225   C
Please send me the book(s) I have checked above.
❑ My check or money order— no cash or CODs please— for $_____is enclosed (please add $1.50 to cover postage and handling for each book ordered— Canadian residents add 7% GST).
❑ Charge my VISA/MC Acct#_____Exp Date_____
Minimum credit card order is two books or $6.00 (please add postage and handling charge of $1.50 per book — Canadian residents add 7% GST). For faster service, call 1-800-762-0779. Residents of Tennessee, please call 1-800-633-1607. Prices and numbers are subject to change without notice. Please allow six to eight weeks for delivery.

Name_____
Address_____
City_____State/Zip_____
Telephone No._____   HOT 0395

The Groundbreaking #1
New York Times Bestseller by
ADELE FABER & ELAINE MAZLISH

"Have I got a book for you!...Run, don't walk, to your nearest bookstore."
Ann Landers

SIBLINGS WITHOUT RIVALRY
How to Help Your Children Live Together So You Can Live Too
70527-3/$10.00 US/$12.00 Can

Don't miss their landmark book

HOW TO TALK SO KIDS WILL LISTEN AND LISTEN SO KIDS WILL TALK
57000-9/$11.00 US/$15.00 Can

"Will get more cooperation from children than all the yelling and pleading in the world." *Christian Science Monitor*

and also

LIBERATED PARENTS, LIBERATED CHILDREN
71134-6/$10.00 US/$12.00 Can

Buy these books at your local bookstore or use this coupon for ordering:

Mail to: Avon Books, Dept BP, Box 767, Rte 2, Dresden, TN 38225   C
Please send me the book(s) I have checked above.
❑ My check or money order— no cash or CODs please— for $_____ is enclosed (please add $1.50 to cover postage and handling for each book ordered— Canadian residents add 7% GST).
❑ Charge my VISA/MC Acct#_____Exp Date_____
Minimum credit card order is two books or $6.00 (please add postage and handling charge of $1.50 per book — Canadian residents add 7% GST). For faster service, call 1-800-762-0779. Residents of Tennessee, please call 1-800-633-1607. Prices and numbers are subject to change without notice. Please allow six to eight weeks for delivery.

Name_____
Address_____
City_____ State/Zip_____
Telephone No._____   FM 0395